# BATTLE

## IN THE

## CIVIL WAR

Paddy Griffith

*Illustrated by*

## Peter Dennis

FIELD
BOOKS

--- CONTENTS ---

Published by Fieldbooks, 47 Owlsmoor Road, Camberley, Surrey GU15 4SW
© Copyright 1986 Fieldbooks. All rights reserved.

ISBN 1  86  9871  00  6

# PART ONE : THE ARMY COMMANDER'S PROBLEM

# THE STRATEGY OF THE CIVIL WAR

The war started when the southern states seceded from the Union and started to evict Federal garrisons by force. Jefferson Davis became the Confederate president, with his government in Richmond. As a former West Pointer and ex-US Secretary of War he possessed a sound grasp of strategy and the needs of armies, although his organizational talents were rather less obvious. He tried to run rather too much of the war single-handed, with the result that the central Confederate staff in Richmond was considerably less efficient than its Northern counterpart in Washington DC.

Davis knew the Confederacy was badly outnumbered in both manpower and industrial resources. If it had to fight a long war it would almost certainly be doomed to defeat - unless it could make an alliance with one of the European great powers. The best hope therefore lay in winning spectacular early victories which would convince the North that there was no point in continuing the fight. Davis was not trying to invade or destroy the North - merely to exert pressure which would lead to a quick peace settlement or at least to European intervention.

**In the far West** the vast distances meant only small forces could be supported. The Union early secured Missouri at the battle of Pea Ridge, but failed to do much good on the Red River in either 1863 or 1864, despite capturing much of Arkansas by the end of 1863. By the end of the war they had also landed troops on the Mexican border as part of the blockade.

**The Confederacy** was difficult to defe because Union forces could approach almost anywhere along some 4,000 miles frontier, by land or sea. The southern n was far too small, and internal rail and ri communications were either decrepit or vulnerable to attack. The defenders we spread thin against multiple spearheads converging against them, yet they were usually fighting on their home ground. E effective strategy they could often conce trate their forces at a key point.

**On the Mississippi** in 1862 Butler captured New Orleans from the South while Halleck sent riverine forces downstream from St. Louis. Ulysses S Grant was successful at Fort Donelson but was then surprised and almost beaten at Shiloh on the Tennessee. Operations became stalled before the Confederate fortresses at Vicksburg and Port Hudson until they fell in mid-1863. This secured the Mississippi for the Union and split the Confederacy in two.

**In the Tennessee Bend** after Shiloh Halleck cautiously approached Corinth but allowed Bragg to raid north first to Perryville and then to Murfreesboro. In both cases the Union general Rosecrans avoided disaster, but losses were high and there was a breathing space until the battle of Chickamauga late in 1863. There Longstreet's arrival secured a southern victory but Thomas' rearguard stand prevented pursuit. The North regained the initiative at Chattanooga when Grant arrived and defeated Bragg in turn. In 1864 Sherman was able to push on to Atlanta against the cautious Johnston, provoking his replacement by the reckless Hood. Hood lost many men in fruitless counterattacks and then in a disastrous raid north to Nashville against Thomas. Meanwhile Sherman broke out south from Atlanta for a massive scorched earth raid to Savannah, Columbia and on into North Carolina.

# THE COURSE OF THE WAR

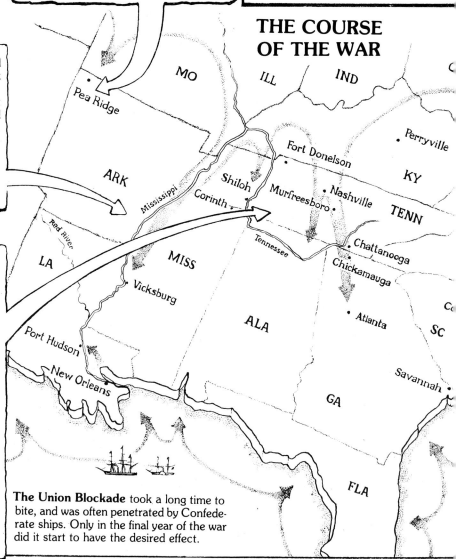

**The Union Blockade** took a long time to bite, and was often penetrated by Confederate ships. Only in the final year of the war did it start to have the desired effect.

**The Union** problem was that each army had to advance into hostile territory at the end of a long supply line. Not only did it have the difficult tactical task of dislodging the enemy from strong defensive positions, but it also had to keep itself fed and equipped. Often this meant detaching large numbers of men to protect rail lines, convoys and rear area depots. The Confederates were often able to disrupt Union plans by launching deep raids against such installations.

**In the East,** unlike in the West, the Confederates early won a clear moral supremacy over their opponents, at the battle of First Manassas, 1861. Next year the Union general McClellan wasted his advantages by a cautious policy in his Peninsula campaign on the Chickahominy, and eventually withdrew from the Richmond area. When the braggart Pope came forward he in turn was defeated at Second Manassas by the deadly Confederate trio of Lee, Jackson and Longstreet, with JEB Stuart's cavalry literally running rings around the Northern army. Lee now raided north to Antietam, but the cautious McClellan again failed to destroy him. Then at Fredericksburg it was Burnside's turn to launch an attack, but this was easily defeated. So was Hooker's flank march to Chancellorsville early in 1863. His Army of the Potomac felt outclassed by Lee's Army of Northern Virginia, and could win only the defensive battle of Gettysburg - this time under the solid if unenterprising Meade. A period of stalemate followed, which Grant failed to break when he took overall command in the spring of 1864. After heavy losses in a series of frontal attacks he arrived outside Petersburg, where a ten month siege was the only result. Victory was postponed until April 1865 when a lightning campaign up the Appomattox river, spearheaded by Sheridan's dashing cavalry, finally broke Lee's once-unbeatable army.

Abraham Lincoln, the Union president, was a civilian with only very slight military experience. His skill lay in political manipulation rather than in strategy, although he learned fast as the war went on. Lincoln came into conflict with many of his generals, who resented what they felt was excessive political interference. They were also suspicious of the administrative centralisation introduced by businessmen like Secretary of War Stanton. Nevertheless it was civilian organisation and efficiency at the top which gave the Union an important advantage over their opponents.

At the start of the war the military professionals wanted Lincoln to adopt a slow cautious strategy. This was called the 'Anaconda Plan', designed to strangle the Confederacy by naval blockade and control of the Mississippi river line. Political pressure soon called for a direct frontal assault on Richmond, however, so the war turned into a struggle at close quarters, instead.

**The end of the war** finally came about as a result neither of frontal assaults wearing down the Confederates, nor of the stand-off 'Anaconda' blockading. It took both of these, plus deep raiding against southern communications and industries before the Union was restored. Fire as well as the sword had to be used, which made the war far more bitter and destructive than if it could have been settled by a few quick battles.

The war lasted so long because the weaker side won the early rounds in the decisive Eastern theatre, but lacked the strength to convert these victories into a peace settlement. The Union was not wounded mortally, but could stay in the fight over the longer haul, and in the long haul the South stood no chance.

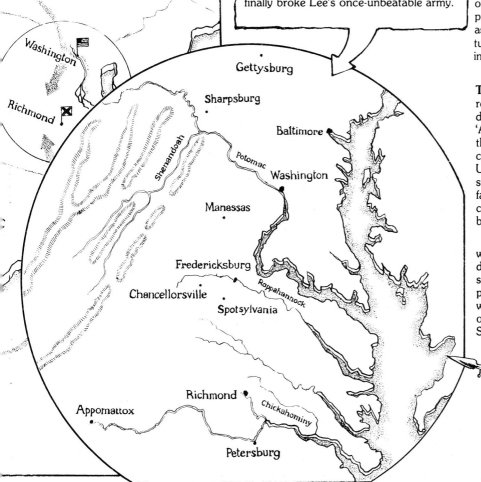

# THE ARMY COMMANDER'S PROBLEM

When an army commander arrived in his theater of operations he had to collect his army, assess the strategic needs and form a plan of action. If what he wanted to do conflicted with the views of his government, he could use negotiation, obstruction or private initiative to win his point - but he might still be overruled.

The essential thing was to make sure the troops were ready for hard marching and fighting, and had sufficient supplies and transport to keep them going. The commander also needed to know what type of maneuvers he wanted to use - a lightning 'Napoleonic' campaign, or a more cautious approach?

**Basic Considerations :** Have we a chance to advance against the enemy, or is he advancing against us? Who has the superior force, and by how much? What is the state of terrain and the importance of the theater to the national war effort? Is is worth risking battle, or should we play safe and win delays without heavy losses? These are the types of questions which shape a campaign.

**EXAMPLE :** In spring of 1862 McClellan collected a large army near Washington and felt he could risk some of it to attack Richmond. But he believed (wrongly, in fact) that he was outnumbered by the enemy, so he did not press his attack hard. His objective was vital for the war, but the imagined odds and the difficult terrain reduced the commander's desire for battle.

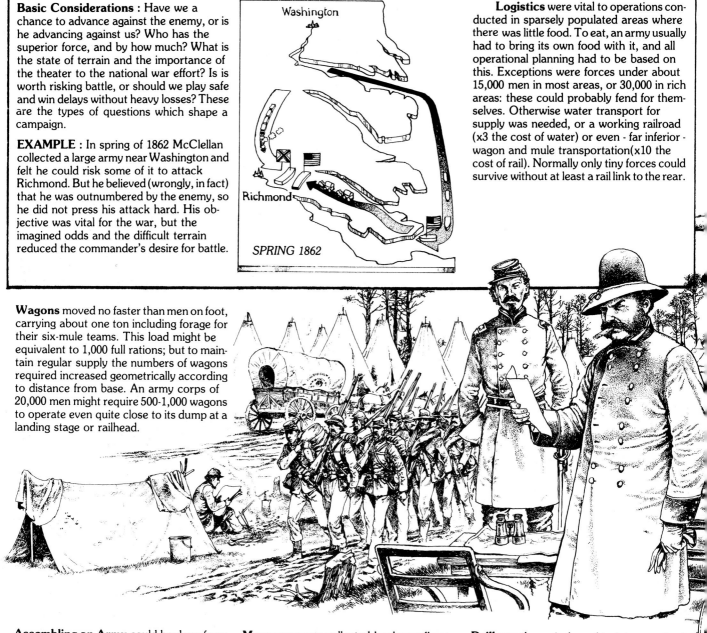

*SPRING 1862*

**Logistics** were vital to operations conducted in sparsely populated areas where there was little food. To eat, an army usually had to bring its own food with it, and all operational planning had to be based on this. Exceptions were forces under about 15,000 men in most areas, or 30,000 in rich areas: these could probably fend for themselves. Otherwise water transport for supply was needed, or a working railroad (x3 the cost of water) or even - far inferior - wagon and mule transportation(x10 the cost of rail). Normally only tiny forces could survive without at least a rail link to the rear.

**Wagons** moved no faster than men on foot, carrying about one ton including forage for their six-mule teams. This load might be equivalent to 1,000 full rations; but to maintain regular supply the numbers of wagons required increased geometrically according to distance from base. An army corps of 20,000 men might require 500-1,000 wagons to operate even quite close to its dump at a landing stage or railhead.

**Assembling an Army** could be done from local resources (eg in 1861 the Virginia militia operated on the Potomac and the Missouri militia moved to the Arkansas border) or by centrally-determined concentrations (eg Burnside's corps was sent from Virginia to North Carolina in 1863, then to Kentucky and then Mississippi. Meanwhile Longstreet's corps was doing something similar in the South). Usually there was a mixture of both systems, giving a degree of cross-fertilisation between East and West.

**Manpower** was collected haphazardly at first, but by 1862 both sides used a system of volunteers for three years - later supplemented by some conscripts. Most Civil War soldiers went willingly to war, spent 3-12 months becoming acclimatized (and sifting out the temperamentally unfit); then perhaps a year soldiering hard before fatigue and war-weariness set in. Any given army would contain a mixture of regiments each at a different stage in this evolution, although the later it was in the war, the more regiments would have passed their peak.

**Drill** was the main formal training received by the recruit, rarely supplemented by target practice or realistic tactical exercises. Few veteran soldiers were available to add essential words of advice which might have brought the drill books to life - since in the Civil War the armies were improvised from scratch and the learning process was less thorough than if regiments had started with *cadres* of experienced men. Discipline was never fully understood in the European sense - but many units did at least become very good at drill!

**The Theory of Maneuvers -** Offensives can be either **Raids** (mobile, disruptive, but lacking sound logistics and therefore not permanent - *eg* Sherman marching to the sea) or **Invasions** (where progress may be slow but supposed to be for keeps - *eg* Halleck's capture of Corinth). They may be on **Interior Lines** (a small force tries to engage fragments of the enemy separately - *eg* Jackson's Valley campaign 1862), **Exterior Lines** (a large force tries to envelop and cut off the enemy - *eg* Hooker at Chancellorsville or **Frontal** (unsubtle pounding, for which a superiority of force is recommended - *eg* Burnside at Fredericksburg). In this war there was a marked preference for the attack on exterior lines, even with inferior forces (*eg* Lee's Gettysburg campaign).

*Hooker's enveloping move*

Chancellorsville

*Confederate fluid defense on interior lines*

Fredericksburg

A defensive can be **Linear** (*eg* 53 miles of trenches covering Petersburg) or **Fluid** (*eg* Confederate delaying actions in depth before Richmond, 1862, followed by repeated counter-attacks), **Fabian** (a pure delaying/attritional process - *eg* Johnston before Atlanta) or entirely **Counter-Offensive** (*eg* Hood at Atlanta).

Within all these variations there is room for **Feints** (*eg* Sherman many times in his late campaigns) and **Secondary** operations to secure a flank or split the enemy (*eg* Lee near Richmond detached Jackson in 1862 and Early in 1864 to demonstrate in the Shenandoah Valley).

**River Steamers** came in all sizes, but most had a basic speed of 5-10 knots and a payload similar to that of a train. Current was of central importance, since the Mississippi flows around three and a half knots at New Orleans and five and a half at Vicksburg (depending on season). But a steamer could keep up its speed hour after hour for days on end, and was far preferable to a railroad. The Union seizure of the main rivers early in the war closed this means of transportation to the Confederates, however.

**Railroads** were better built and more reliable in North than South, but had to cover longer distances on exterior lines. Especially in the South wrecks were quite frequent, as were delays to change company or guage. A train normally carried 500-1,000 men or 100 tons of supplies, and although it might reach a speed of 25 mph or more, an overall average of 150 miles in 24 hours was considered fast for large scale movements.

**Camp Life** was the informal part of a recruit's training, teaching him to live outdoors - under tents or bivouacs on campaign,or home made log dugouts for winter quarters. He would learn to husband his rations and cook them, as well as to get along with his comrades and officers. To many this was all a shock too severe to stand, and a regiment might lose half its strength to all causes before it became fully acclimated to army life. But those who were left would be fit for any service.

**Morale** had to be built by officers winning the trust of their men. They had to provide adequate rations and a sense of purpose, if not always of confidence in victory. Mail and newspapers were important to morale, as was the avoidance of excessively harsh punishments. But as in all armies, it was ultimately the army commander's responsibility to build morale by demonstrating to his troops that he was competent. He had to delay entering the field until his army was trained and ready, and when he did open his campaign he had to maneuver with at least a basic minimum of skill.

**Fortification** was a common duty for troops waiting to enter a campaign, and the Americans habitually erected massive earthworks around their depots and major centers, right from the start of the war. This was partly because most army commanders had been trained at West Point - a school of engineering - but also perhaps because inexperienced armies with inexperienced leaders required particularly strong reassurances that they wound not be surprised by an enemy attack. The major uncertainty facing any army, in fact, was to know what was happening in the opponent's camp 'on the other side of the hill'.

# FINDING THE ENEMY

The army commander drew upon two intelligence nets - his own, within his army (featured here); and the general national net run by his central government (which would feed him mainly strategic background information). Since this was a *civil* war, and both sides spoke the same language, strategic information was relatively easy to come by. Local tactical information, by contrast, posed many more problems.

Generals could often see deep into the minds of their opponent, due to long acquaintance at West Point and in the Mexican war of 1846-8. But in the wooded undulating terrain of the Civil War it was often difficult to see deep into the enemy army. A force which eluded surveillance could move rapidly in an unexpected direction, to emerge triumphantly on flank or rear (eg Jackson at Second Manassas, Longstreet at Chickamauga). Probably fewer commanders took advantage of this possibility than might have done - but all were aware of the vital need to watch every move their opponent made, by using every available means of collecting intelligence.

**Signal Stations** were set up in an interlocking grid throughout a theater of operations. Their primary role was to pass messages by semaphore ('wig wag') within the friendly army; but their location on hilltops also gave them an ideal opportunity to report enemy movements (eg the Confederate wig wag gave the first warning of the Union flank attack at First Manassas). They could also intercept messages passed by enemy wig wags. A cipher war therefore developed between opposing signal stations. This was won by the Union in 1863 when the Myer cipher disc was introduced, although it was never as widely used as it ought to have been - 'for security reasons'.

**Balloons** were used extensively by the Union early in the war, then largely discontinued as not cost-effective. Although they might not see all that much, they did force the enemy to take costly counter-measures and it is arguable that they were more valuable to the North than was realized at the time.

**Cavalry Pickets** were not quite as expert and dedicated in intelligence work as signal stations, but they could roam more widely and gain a closer 'worm's eye' view of the situation. They were actually the major source of information in most Civil War armies, and it was therefore essential for a commander to achieve supremacy in the cavalry outpost line. At the start of the war the Confederates usually enjoyed this supremacy, but it gradually slipped from their grasp.

Cavalry sent out to collect intelligence would advance in small groups with heavy supports behind, ready to run if outnumbered or reinforce if they could push through. With modern binoculars they could distinguish details at a mile that might otherwise be clear only at 500 yards. But if they lacked maps or the opportunity to count individuals (eg crossing a bridge) they might still get lost or give misleading returns.

myer's disc

**Analysing the Information** was largely a matter for the individual army commander and perhaps a trusted specialist personally appointed for the task. General McClellan trusted the detective Pinkerton too far and received badly exaggerated analyses; General Sherman did his own intelligence work, often more effectively than his subordinates. Hooker and Meade used a reliable staff to process and sift all the reports they received. There was no standardised organization for this branch, such as we know today. A great deal depended on the commander's military insight into the strengths his opponent could keep supplied, the practicalities of different courses of action and the state of mind of the enemy officers and men.

**Infantry Pickets** had a different character from the cavalry, since they were closely tied to the perimeter of the army, and did not roam widely. Indeed, the army's position was effectively defined by the position of its infantry outposts during each night's camp.

Infantry pickets had no special training for gathering intelligence, but they would often exchange banter - and trade desirable products - with their opposite numbers on the enemy side. Federals brought coffee, Confederates brought tobacco; both brought newspapers and personal opinions. The result was a free interchange of military news which could give the pickets an accurate view of the local situation.

There were two problems: in the first place the news thus transmitted might be little better than rumor, even when it didn't come out of a newspaper. Secondly the news might never find its way further back than the picket itself, or at least the regiment from which it was drawn. Picket news filtered back to the army commander in an erratic and unreliable way.

**Interrogation of Prisoners** could usually produce a lot of valuable information, provided there was an efficient system for collecting and distributing it. The armies achieved such a system only about half way through the war, especially when Hooker in the Army of the Potomac set up a Bureau of Military Information.

**Scouts and Spies** were particularly common in this war, since there was no language barrier and almost anyone could pose as a supporter of the other side. There were also many sympathisers resident beyond the enemy lines, who could offer shelter and an *alibi*. A daring man could always creep or bluff his way through enemy pickets, claiming to be a civilian, a deserter or a friendly soldier - even an officer. At best such spies could collect important headquarter news, although usually they would simply see a little deeper into the enemy camp, locally, than could the regular pickets.

**Countermeasures** were used by all armies, to block enemy intelligence gathering. Routes were chosen, as far as possible, to avoid the line of sight from opposition balloons and signal stations - and this often meant wide diversions.

Countermeasures against cavalry were difficult unless your own cavalry was sufficiently strong and active to attack the enemy's patrols wherever they appeared, and persuade him it was best to stay at home.

Various ruses were tried at different times to confuse infantry pickets - eg an abandoned position might be left with camp fires burning, straw men representing sentries and treetrunks for cannon ("Quaker guns"). The idea would be to win time by concealing your move to the next position. On other occasions a few troops might be marched round and round in the enemy's sight, to create the impression of superior numbers. It was a trick which sometimes even worked, particularly for the Confederate cavalry leader Nathan B Forrest.

Prisoners of war sometimes gave misleading information - or no information at all - to their captors. Scouts and spies who were caught were often executed to discourage the others. But by and large there was no sure-fire way of preventing gossip and information seeping across the battle line to the enemy. Sometimes a movement could be completed undetected, but at other times it would have to put up with continuous surveillance.

**Strategic Information** came from outside the army and could take many forms - intelligence from the national telegraph net and from wire taps; information from diplomats, merchants or refugees; analyses of enemy newspapers; general political background and careerist gossip from civilian politicians and military staff officers. All of this could be of great value to a field commander in helping him to understand the higher context of his operations, although it might not often help him to plan his day by day maneuvers against the local enemy. There were exceptions to this, such as when

warning was received of reinforcements due to arrive from another theater.

Union Secretary of War Stanton ran a highly efficient central telegraph office in Washington DC which kept him informed of what each army was doing, and hence allowed each to keep abreast of events nationwide. In Richmond there was never such a good central system, although perhaps there was less need for one since the Northern newspapers often gave away most of what was going on.

# MARCH MANEUVERS

When an army left its base to move against the enemy it would have to choose its roads carefully for both their *direction* in relation to the opponent and their *capacity* to carry troops and vehicles. Each road had to carry enough forces to sustain quite a long independent battle if attacked, but not too many to create traffic jams stretching too far to the rear. Marching men occupied 2-3 times the distance from front to back as they occupied in line of battle from flank to flank. Therefore the more men on each road, the longer the delay before the rearmost could come into action. Ideally the army would use small columns on several roads, so all could come into action at the same time. The poor availability of roads, however, often made this hard to achieve. If roads went in the wrong direction, or were too far apart for mutual support, or were of poor surface quality, the commander would have to make compromises with the ideal. In January 1863 Burnside's move round Lee's flank became - literally - 'stuck in the mud'. At Beaver Dam Creek in June 1862 Lee's two attacking corps were too far apart to co-ordinate their action.

**Travelling Light** was the only way the infantryman on the march could keep going. Anything not absolutely vital was jettisoned early in his campaigning life - clean sheets, 'secondary armament', even religious texts over and above the essential minimum. The weak or the unwilling soon found ways to fall out of the line of march, despite stringent disciplinary arrangements to prevent them. For the rest, the gruelling routine of marching, foraging, scrounging firewood and a suitable site for a shelter tent produced hardened soldiers but often hungry and demoralized ones. Shoe leather, fresh vegetables and a time to relax were all in short supply. The bitterly cold and muddy roads in winter and spring, the oppresively hot and dusty roads in summer and fall - all took their toll of the soldier, who might have to carry 40-60 pounds of equpment.It is not surprising that standards of honesty towards civilian hens and fence-rails were soon eroded; that many infantrymen aspired to become cavalry (a few even succeeded); or that 'march losses' were often higher than combat casualties. The real veterans of this war had to survive at least thirty six months of such a nomadic existence before they could win their discharge.

**Order of March :** The army advances on several roads, with one or more army corps on each road. Each corps has an advance guard to lead the way, and a main body to do the hard work. The latter is composed mostly of infantry, artillery and baggage - including the bulk of the HQ staff, beef on the hoof and the wagons. Normally infantry take the lead with artillery following near the baggage park. The rearguard is an all-arms force with provost troops to pick up stragglers.

**Column Lengths:** According to the drill book a column of fours had one yard between men, hence 1,000 men occupy 250 yards of road. In reality, however, comfortable marching at 'route step, at ease, arms at will' meant that 500-700 yards were needed, plus extra space for attached staff, baggage, cattle and camp followers. Allow the following distances (in miles):-

| Unit | With Baggage | Without Baggage |
|---|---|---|
| Infantry Brigade | 0.8 | 0.6 |
| Division | 4 | 2.5 |
| Corps | 14 | 8 |
| Cavalry Brigade | 1.5 | 1 |
| Division | 6 | 4 |
| Artillery Battery | 0.3 | 0.2 |
| Army HQ and Staff | 3 | - |
| Army parks, reserve ammunition &c | 15 (but very variable) | - |

**The Marching Column** must try to avoid crossing the route of other columns - that would create traffic jams and delays - and must allow time for 'choke points' such as bridges or defiles. As the military situation develops, each column is likely to be re-routed in a new direction - marching to help another column which is in difficulties, perhaps, or moving around the flank of a newly-identified enemy force. The commander of each column must be especially alert to the changing needs - otherwise great opportunities may be lost.

**The Advance Guard** is a mixed force of cavalry, horse artillery and lightly-equipped infantry under an enterprising commander. If possible it is preceded by deep reconnaissance and cavalry scouts to warn of the enemy's presence. Pioneers, staff officers and quartermasters go along too, to prepare the way for the main body's march.

**Contact** takes place when the head of a marching column bumps the enemy. Much will depend on the latter's intentions. Is he advancing to attack or covering a withdrawal? The answers will determine whether this builds up into a major action or fizzles out quickly. The advance guard commander must make a decision to press forward or wait, and the commander of the whole force must also decide whether he can crack this opposition with his own resources, or whether he must call in help from another force.

If the enemy is strong and holds firm, then we have here the beginnings of a full scale battle!

**The Position of The General** in the line of march depends on his style of leadership. An energetic corpos commander may travel close behind his advance guard, to keep up to date with what was going on. A wise army commander may choose the most important road and follow the advance guard of the leading corps upon it.

**Roads** needed constant attention to keep them serviceable during the wet months of the year (December to May, but especially March and April). Corduroy surfaces were needed wherever the mud was deep, let alone bottomless. In some cases, however, the road surface became so liquid that the cords themselves floated away!

**Timetable of the marching day:** Marches started either early in the morning or around dusk. Night marches were sometimes used to deceive the enemy, but were slow, wasteful and hated by the troops. The best marches began with a hearty breakfast at dawn, continued unhindered until a long rest at two-thirds' distance, and ended with a late lunch followed by foraging and camping. But if there were delays, traffic jams or enemy action to contend with, it would be an exhausted and famished soldier who staggered into his bivouac late in the day - or even into the fighting line.

The marching day was usually about eight hours including rests. Precision is inappropriate, but the following schedules would be normal:

| Arm | Speed (miles per hour) | Ability to do more than eight hours |
|---|---|---|
| Infantry Division | 2.5 | good |
| Corps | 2.5(-) | fair |
| Cavalry | 4(+) | poor |
| Horse artillery | 4 | poor |
| Foot artillery | 2.5 | fair |
| Separate wagon train | 2.5(-) | none |

# TRANSMITTING THE COMMANDER'S ORDERS

When the army commander has assembled his army, assessed his intelligence and made a plan, he is ready to issue his orders. Standing instructions and general briefings for the campaign can be circulated at leisure before the troops move out, but once maneuvers are under way the commander will have to use every means in his power to communicate with his troops. Merely passing messages around the army in good time will be a major undertaking - and one of the most vital aspects of staffwork. Obviously an order is useless unless it reaches its destination before being overtaken by events!

**Style** : When writing orders, the commander must choose his style. Does he want to appear as the soldier's buddy and helper - or does he want to appear as an all-seeing higher authority who must be obeyed? The commander who is seen by his troops often will risk losing touch with his own HQ; but the commander who spends too much time running things from the center risks getting cut off from the way his soldiers are thinking. Pope tried to be too popular before his downfall at Second Manassas; Bragg tried to be too demanding before his at Chattanooga.

Orders must be short, legible, unambiguous, informative and - if possible - inspiring. They must say who they are from and when they were sent; to whom they are sent and why. They must state times and places of movements intended, plus as much background as possible - things like general intentions of the army commander, actions by supporting troops, or information about enemy or terrain which the recipient will need. The recipient must be put in the picture as well as spurred into action.

**Signals** were passed mainly by three methods:-

**The Wig Wag** could pass short messages fast across a battlefield if there were not too many intervening trees or clouds. It might need five minutes for each relay - the spacing of the stations being dependent on the terrain.

**The Field Telegraph** sometimes reached nine medium-length messages in an hour, where it was properly set up.

**Couriers** remained the chief means of communication, even in the technological late-war Union armies. Speed and reliability varied enormously, but long orders could usually be distributed quickly - and then explained personally by the courier himself.

**Couriers** could be anyone from an officer's servant sent on a mule to do his best, right up to a dashing young officer using a string of thoroughbreds. One Virginian aristocrat, H Kyd Douglas, once rode 105 miles in 20 hours with a message from Jackson, although half that speed would normally be considered good.

Most couriers were used for only local missions, within the army's area. But without maps, in broken country, they still had difficulty finding their man - who might himself be moving. Even then there would sometimes be difficulty of communication, if the message was not properly written out. The weakness of the courier system was the same as its strength - it was personal and 'word of mouth'.

**The Telegraph in the Field** : The primary role of the electric telegraph was strategic, between the army commander and his central government. But within each army it was also possible to set up telegraphs locally and temporarily, to allow HQ to talk to corps and even (by 1864 in the main Union armies) division commanders. Sherman had field telegraphs operating up to six miles from his HQ. Grant in the Wilderness had a wire-laying mule with each brigade. The Confederates had less of this equipment, and relied more on couriers and the wig wag.

In the early years of the war the field telegraph had not been widespread. Early experiments had failed, and regular use by the Union of the Beardslee system had been limited. It had been useful at Fredericksburg - a static battle where mist obscured the wig wag - but at Chancellorsville events moved too fast for links to be maintained. There was also an institutional problem, since Stanton neglected the field telegraph in favor of strategic lines.

## The Organization of Staffs

**The General's Inner Circle** would be a group of hand-picked officers to run his personal paperwork and 'household', and to ride as couriers.

**The Adjutant General** was really the 'chief of staff' responsible for the army's correspondence, movements, personnel administration, appointments &c. He kept track on operations and might also run intelligence, he co-operated with the staffs of Cavalry, Artillery, Engineers, Topographical Engineers (mapping), Signals &c.

**The Inspector General** was responsible for each unit's efficiency and discipline, backed up by the Provost Marshal (military police) and Judge Advocate (courts martial). Training and doctrine came within the Inspector General's responsibilities, but were rarely developed far beyond basic drill.

**The Quartermaster General** looked after most aspects of supply and transportation, with the Subsistence and Ordnance staffs, the Wagonmasters, Railroad, Medical, Postal and Pay organisations, &c.

**Staffs** varied greatly from army to army but the results were often disappointing, especially in the early years before experience had brought improvements and regularity. Each level of command had representatives of each staff service - eg a brigade might have a quartermaster, a commissary, an adjutant plus a few medics and ADCs; an army corps might have more of each, and at higher ranks, with larger organizations below them. At army level the staffs were bigger still: Meade's HQ at Gettysburg contained 3,486 people, exclusive of artillery and engineer staffs.

**Signalling Times :** The wide variety of terrains and signalling methods make it hard to be definite about timings in any given situation, but as a rough guide allow the following:-

| From | To | Time |
|---|---|---|
| Strategic Information Agencies | Army Commander | 24 Hours |
| Scouts/Spies | Army Commander | 72 Hours |
| Central Government | Army Commander | 24 Hours |
| Outlying Cavalry | Army Commander | 12 Hours |
| Infantry Pickets | Army Commander | 6 Hours |
| Wig Wags/Couriers within army | Army Commander | 1 Hour |
| Army Commander | Corps Commander | 1 Hour |
| Corps HQ | Division HQ | 30 Minutes |
| Division HQ | Brigade HQ | 20 Minutes |
| Brigade HQ | Regimental HQ | 15 Minutes |
| Regimental HQ | Company Commander | 5 Minutes |
| Company Commander | Enlisted Man | 1 Minute |

# PART TWO: THE ARMY COMMANDER'S BATTLE
# DEPLOYING THE ARMY

When a contact leads to a battle, the most important thing for a commander is to deploy his fighting line. His men are vulnerable and powerless while they remain in route column - but once extended into line facing the enemy they can fight at their full value.

The first brigades into action throw forward a screen of skirmishers to occupy the enemy. Behind it the formed regiments make a line to start the battle.

As the remainder of the division arrives it forms additional brigades just behind the front line, to support it. The division will usually fight in two, three or four lines of brigades.

If this is a big battle there may be several more divisions available. The commander must decide whether to place them in line alongside the one which is already engaged, or to mass them in reserve or as a 'battering ram' to break through.

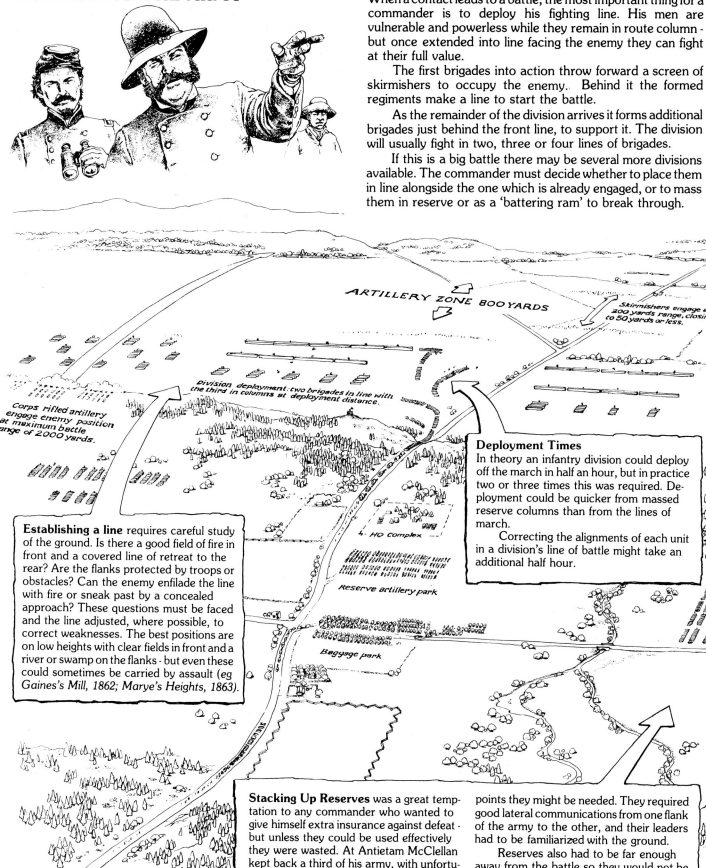

ARTILLERY ZONE 800 YARDS

Skirmishers engage at 200 yards range, closing to 50 yards or less.

Division deployment: two brigades in line with the third in columns at deployment distance.

Corps rifled artillery engage enemy position at maximum battle range of 2000 yards.

4. HQ Complex

Reserve artillery park

Baggage park

**Deployment Times**
In theory an infantry division could deploy off the march in half an hour, but in practice two or three times this was required. Deployment could be quicker from massed reserve columns than from the lines of march.

Correcting the alignments of each unit in a division's line of battle might take an additional half hour.

**Establishing a line** requires careful study of the ground. Is there a good field of fire in front and a covered line of retreat to the rear? Are the flanks protected by troops or obstacles? Can the enemy enfilade the line with fire or sneak past by a concealed approach? These questions must be faced and the line adjusted, where possible, to correct weaknesses. The best positions are on low heights with clear fields in front and a river or swamp on the flanks - but even these could sometimes be carried by assault (eg Gaines's Mill, 1862; Marye's Heights, 1863).

**Stacking Up Reserves** was a great temptation to any commander who wanted to give himself extra insurance against defeat - but unless they could be used effectively they were wasted. At Antietam McClellan kept back a third of his army, with unfortunate results.

Reserves had to be placed in positions from which they could move quickly to the points they might be needed. They required good lateral communications from one flank of the army to the other, and their leaders had to be familiarized with the ground.

Reserves also had to be far enough away from the battle so they would not be involved with it or suffer from too many overshots.

If it is a really big battle, several army corps will be arriving to take part. Once again the commander must decide whether to allocate them to a new line of action, alongside those already fighting, or whether to hold them back for some other purpose.

Many important decisions have to be taken during the deployment of the army, because that is when the commander occupies what he thinks is the important ground and leaves the remainder unclaimed. At Gettysburg the Union forces at first did not think the zone on their left flank was important, and nearly lost the battle as a result. At Chickamauga they inadvertently left a gap in the center of their line - and they did lose the battle.

A line must not be stretched out so far that it is too thinly held and breakable, but neither should too many troops be crammed into a small frontage. That would prevent many of them from fighting at all.

Timing is also vital in the deployment phase. The ideal is to bring the whole army into action simultaneously, in order to get the best out of everyone. If a fraction of the army has to carry the whole battle for too long, it may be broken. If reserves arrive too late, they may miss the battle altogether. The army commander must use foresight and staffwork to make sure they are not too far away when the fighting starts. General Lee was not very good at this trick in the Seven Days battles of 1862, but had mastered it better at Second Manassas.

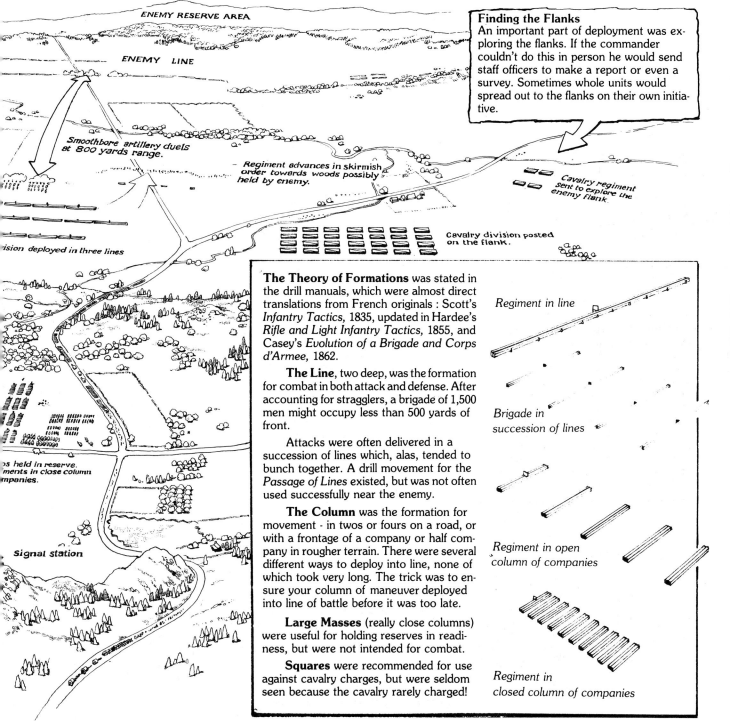

**Finding the Flanks**
An important part of deployment was exploring the flanks. If the commander couldn't do this in person he would send staff officers to make a report or even a survey. Sometimes whole units would spread out to the flanks on their own initiative.

ENEMY RESERVE AREA

ENEMY LINE

Smoothbore artillery duels at 800 yards range.

Regiment advances in skirmish order towards woods possibly held by enemy.

Cavalry regiment sent to explore the enemy flank

Cavalry division posted on the flank.

vision deployed in three lines

s held in reserve. ments in close column mpanies.

Signal station

**The Theory of Formations** was stated in the drill manuals, which were almost direct translations from French originals : Scott's *Infantry Tactics*, 1835, updated in Hardee's *Rifle and Light Infantry Tactics*, 1855, and Casey's *Evolution of a Brigade and Corps d'Armee*, 1862.

**The Line**, two deep, was the formation for combat in both attack and defense. After accounting for stragglers, a brigade of 1,500 men might occupy less than 500 yards of front.

Attacks were often delivered in a succession of lines which, alas, tended to bunch together. A drill movement for the *Passage of Lines* existed, but was not often used successfully near the enemy.

**The Column** was the formation for movement - in twos or fours on a road, or with a frontage of a company or half company in rougher terrain. There were several different ways to deploy into line, none of which took very long. The trick was to ensure your column of maneuver deployed into line of battle before it was too late.

**Large Masses** (really close columns) were useful for holding reserves in readiness, but were not intended for combat.

**Squares** were recommended for use against cavalry charges, but were seldom seen because the cavalry rarely charged!

*Regiment in line*

*Brigade in succession of lines*

*Regiment in open column of companies*

*Regiment in closed column of companies*

# THE BATTLE STARTS

Once the battle has fairly started, the troops in contact with the enemy become to a great extent lost to the army commander. They fight as best they can against the immediate opposition, responding only sluggishly to orders from above - unless these happen to coincide with what they were already doing. At Gettysburg Lee's attempts to hurry up his subordinates' attacks were unsuccessful: at Fredericksburg and Kenesaw the Union front line remained close to the enemy for more than a day after its assault had failed.

**In Open Battle** there were wide fields of fire although Civil War commanders often preferred to reserve their shots until they could be sure of scoring hits. Also, even in the most open ground, there were usually fences, furrows or low ridges behind which prone men could take cover. In the absence of a large battle cavalry to overrun them, such troops were almost as well protected as if they were behind fieldworks. And in any case, open battlefields like Antietam were the exception rather than the rule in this war.

**In Forest Fighting** there was obviously plentiful cover at hand. The trees gave soldiers an opportunity to seek cover in safety, at the same time as they created difficulties of command and control. Woods restricted the use of long range artillery and concealed the development of the action from higher commanders. They gave a specially 'formless' character to the war, and helped prevent the battles from being decisive. Whether at Chickamauga or on the Chickahominy, in the Wilderness or at Wilson's Creek, it was usually the trees which got in the way of brilliant generalship.

**In Swampland Fighting** the normal problems of forest warfare were complicated by the high water table. In the Mississippi bayous and in some of Sherman's final battles the soldiers often had to wade waist deep to come into action. In winter, also, even normally 'firm' ground on the other battlefields could easily turn to thick, clinging mud. Troops who had to lie prone would instantly become caked in it from head to foot, while the movement of guns or wagons would turn into a major problem of engineering.

**Fieldworks** were often built in the Civil War, right from the start of hostilities. They were deemed to add solidity and reassurance to mass armies of 'civilians in uniform' who would be very shaky in the open field. Unfortunately fieldworks came to be a habit with Civil War soldiers, even after they had learned solidity under fire. By the end of the war it was widely believed that fortifications were essential to all operations, which made it harder than ever to fight battles of mobility and maneuver. They helped the action to bog down still further.

**The Inferno** of battle in the Civil War was no worse than what had been seen in Napoleonic times - the scale of casualties was roughly comparable - but in the 1860s there was the added demoralizing factor that the battles rarely seemed to achieve anything useful. Major attacks did not often win their objectives but more usually led to a 'slaughter pen', where massed bodies of attackers in open ground had to suffer heavy close range fire from defenders sitting behind fortifications. At Antietam - 'America's bloodiest day' - the Union attack was a failure, but a total of 22,000 men of the two sides had been killed or wounded within twelve short hours. At Cold Harbor two years later Grant's attack was just as unsuccessful and he lost 6,000 men in an hour. At the Petersburg Crater the Union loss was 4,000 in the same timescale, and Grant called it 'The saddest affair I have witnessed in the war'.

The Confederates were no less likely than the Northerners to send their men into a 'slaughter pen', and modern scholarship has shown that their attacking energy early in the war actually made them more likely. In repeated assaults in the Seven Days battles of 1862 they lost some 20,000 men, and only one Union position was captured. In Pickett's charge at Gettysburg about a half

of the 15,000 assault troops were hit, for no tactical benefit.

The problem for Civil War commanders was that a massed frontal attack often seemed to be the only way to get a decisive result, even though it was expensive. To attack in a half-hearted way, or to go round a

flank, was to risk a defeat - or at least it allowed the enemy to sneak away. And besides, unsubtle offensive tactics did sometimes work. At Missionary Ridge, Chattanooga, Grant successfully carried an exceptionally strong fortified position simply by marching up it in a massed frontal assault!

## SOME EXAMPLES

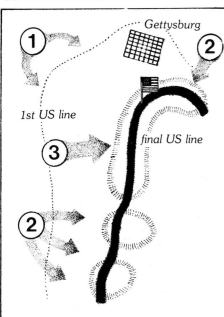

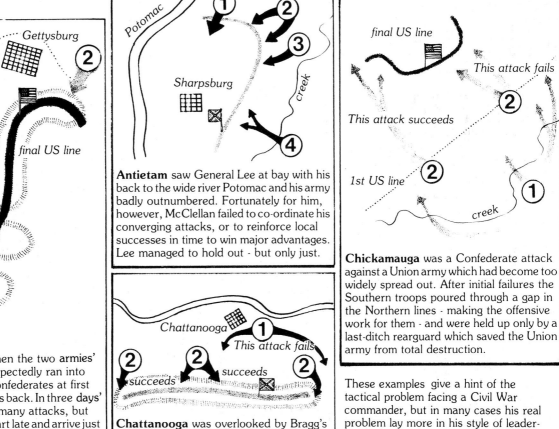

**Gettysburg** began when the two armies' advanced guards unexpectedly ran into each other and the Confederates at first pushed the Northerners back. In three days' fighting Lee launched many attacks, but each one seemed to start late and arrive just after Meade had reinforced his defensive positions. Nevertheless the Union forces, which outnumbered the Confederates, were sufficiently impressed to stay on the defensive and allow Lee to retire gracefully.

**Antietam** saw General Lee at bay with his back to the wide river Potomac and his army badly outnumbered. Fortunately for him, however, McClellan failed to co-ordinate his converging attacks, or to reinforce local successes in time to win major advantages. Lee managed to hold out - but only just.

**Chattanooga** was overlooked by Bragg's fortifications on Missionary Ridge, which unexpectedly collapsed under a well co-ordinated Union assault. As so often, however, a rearguard managed to save the defeated army from total destruction.

**Chickamauga** was a Confederate attack against a Union army which had become too widely spread out. After initial failures the Southern troops poured through a gap in the Northern lines - making the offensive work for them - and were held up only by a last-ditch rearguard which saved the Union army from total destruction.

These examples give a hint of the tactical problem facing a Civil War commander, but in many cases his real problem lay more in his style of leadership and the ways that his heavy responsibilities weighed upon him. The true test of generalship in battle was not so much what the general wanted to do but the way he made it happen.

# GENERALSHIP IN BATTLE

Once he has made his dispositions for battle, the army commander has to work hard to keep it going in the direction he wants : he must shape the course of events all the way through.

This means he must keep in touch with what is happening at the front, with the status of his own and the enemy's reserves, and with 'the big picture'. He must not get sucked too far into an unfavorable battle, but must not hold back from one which might turn into a decisive victory.

**The General As Hero.** Everyone likes to think of the general as an heroic figure with complete foresight before the event and total knowledge of what is happening during it. He will always be where he is needed most, and will snap out wonderfully precise and relevant orders exactly on time. His personal charisma and self-confidence will evoke complete obedience from his subordinates.

**The Reality**, however, was that many commanders succumbed under the strain, and even successful ones experienced a level of stress which tested their personalities to the limit. In the crisis of each battle they found themselves blinded by the fog of war, battered by the unreasonable demands of their superiors and subordinates, frustrated by the basic inability of Civil War armies to do the right thing as quickly as the textbooks seemed to think they should. Command in battle was often a matter of making life-and-death decisions on the basis of wild guesses or, at best, half-informed hunches.

In these circumstances it is scarcely surprising that many commanders exhibited signs of acute stress and tension by the end of the war. Robert E Lee and William T Sherman both seemed to have aged by

some twenty years between 1861 and 1865 - and Sherman, at least, suffered some scarcely sane fits of glorying in destruction. Ulysses S Grant coped with the pressure by occasional bouts of heavy drinking - and we are told that he was by no means unusual in this. In the excitement of combat Philip H Sheridan snapped out a chain of impetuous, contradictory orders which only his personal charisma saved from complete incomprehensibility. 'Stonewall' Jackson became introverted and over-secretive, sucking a lemon and criticising the least failure of regularity, but confusing his subordinates by his failure to let them share his plans.

Sometimes there were open arguments between commanders at key moments - Jackson actually resigned at one point in his Valley campaign, and had to be wooed back

very delicately. Warren and Sheridan fell out at Five Forks; Grant and Halleck at Corinth, Hood and Johnston before Atlanta. The common backgrounds of most generals gave them a pretty good idea of each other's personalities and weaknesses - and tempted them to regard themselves as morally equal even to their legal superiors. Long familiarity did not therefore always breed close co-operation under the strains of combat, nor did a common danger always make lifelong rivals bury their differences.

This familiarity also extended across the battle lines, since Northern generals often had long personal acquaintance with their Southern opponents - eg. in one Mexican war reconnaissance (1846) the four young officers who went forward together were called Jeff Davis, Bob Lee, Sam Grant and George Meade ...

## The General's Checklist

### 1) The Military Situation

Do I know all I need to about the terrain?
Do I know the enemy's position?

- his strength?
- his intentions?

What is my own intention in this battle?
Have I enough troops to achieve it?
Can they get to the right places at the right time?
Will the price they have to pay be too great for the importance of my aim?
Have I adequate reserves in case something goes wrong?
Have I enough time to achieve this (eg how near is nightfall)?
Have I adequate logistics to achieve this? Food? Ammunition?
When can I expect the situation to change, and will I be well placed to respond?

### 2) Staffwork

Are situation reports coming through from my subordinates on time?
Are my orders being obeyed?
Are movements being completed on time?
Are supplies reaching their destinations on time?
Have I adequate signalling facilities with everyone?
Will there be specialist tasks to prepare (eg engineers to lay bridges, artillery to make a concentration)?

### 3) Morale

Are the men confident in victory? Are their officers?
Am I sticking to my original aim?
Am I being as bold as the situation demands?
Am I being as cautious as the situation demands?
Will I be able to face the President/the people/the press/myself with a clear conscience when all this is over?

If there is any doubt about favorable answers to any of these questions, the general must go back and do something to remove it. If there is a favorable reply to each one he must go back and double-check, because that will be a miracle!

If he wants to find out more about what's happening, the commander may go to the front to see for himself - especially to subordinate HQs, but also perhaps nearer the firing. This can be personally risky - but still more important is that it puts the general out of touch with his own staff and signallers.

In desperate circumstances the commander may go right into the fighting itself - to lead a vital charge or rally a unit cracking at a key point. Because of their inferior numbers and more energetic military style, it was usually the Confederate high command which took this risk. Their loss was very heavy - A S Johnston, Jackson, Polk, J E B Stuart, A P Hill, Cleburne and many more were killed in action. No less than twelve Confederate generals were killed, wounded or captured at the battle of Franklin alone.

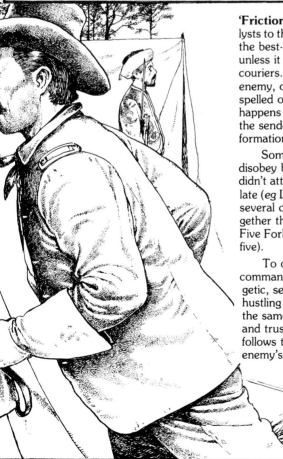

**'Friction'** is the name given by military analysts to the way things can go wrong in even the best-laid plan. An order may not arrive unless it has been sent by several different couriers. It may be intercepted by the enemy, or it may not be obeyed unless spelled out very clearly and the recipient happens to be in the position assumed by the sender. Orders based on incorrect information may be legimately overruled.

Sometimes the recipient of orders may disobey because he disagrees (Warren didn't attack at Mine Run), or he may obey late (eg Longsteet's delay at Gettysburg). If several conflicting orders are issued together there will also be a problem (before Five Forks Warren received no less than five).

To overcome such friction the army commander must be very active and energetic, seeing that orders are obeyed and hustling his reluctant subordinates. Yet at the same time he must keep their respect and trust .. and all at the same time as he follows the course of the battle and the enemy's moves!

More insidious, but perhaps more likely than honorable 'suicide' under fire, was a general's loss of purpose. At Chancellorsville Hooker 'lost faith in Hooker' and failed to carry through the victory he held in his grasp. At Petersburg Butler threw away all his trumps and at Fredericksburg Burnside delayed his attack for vital days. In almost all his battles McClellan gave up when he was winning, just because the Confederate attacks seemed so frenzied.

# CONTROLLING THE BATTLE

One of the most important ways an army commander shapes a battle once it has been started is by the effective use of reserves. The troops already fighting in the front line are to a great extent lost to him - it is the troops not yet in action which can still intervene powerfully, either to increase the pressure in the existing fight, or to open a new front.

The army commander must make sure he always has something in reserve - preferably an all-arms , rested force of veteran troops; but if not, then whatever is available. He must also 'read the battle' to see whether the enemy has a reserve still in hand - or whether the enemy is entirely committed to action. The potentially most successful battles are those which exhaust the enemy's reserves without making inroads into our own. In the Civil War this was achieved several times (eg by Lee at Fredericksburg, Hooker at Chancellorsville, McClellan at Antietam, Meade at Gettysburg &c), but it was rare for this *potentially* devastating position to be turned into an annihilation of the enemy army. For various reasons the successful commanders in the battles named above all preferred not to use their reserves at the psychological moment.

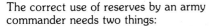

The correct use of reserves by an army commander needs two things:

a) The boldness and determination to stake all at the time and place where he thinks the enemy is vulnerable.

b) An understanding of 'the intelligent use of the three arms' - Reserves should be understood not simply as 'forces to be thrown in', but as a subtle mix of infantry, artillery and cavalry which will together be able to achieve much more than the sum of its parts.

**Infantry** was the basic combat arm of the Civil War and was used in almost every role - often without much help from artillery or cavalry. It was not usually trained for a specifically 'reserve' function, however, as Napoleon's Imperial Guard had been. Most infantry received the same training, although of course a commander would know that some outfits were more reliable than others. The 'Stonewall Brigade' won its reputation at First Manassas for standing firm as a last reserve. 'Iron' and 'Gibralter' brigades were named for similar reasons. On the other side of the coin were the notorious Germans of the Union XI Corps, who mishandled the use of reserves at Chancellorsville, ran off in panic and gained a reputation for running in every battle thereafter.

**Cavalry** was the 'Cinderella' of the Civil War armies, partly because its proper battlefield use was misunderstood, but partly also because it preferred an independent strategic role. In any case cavalry tactics in battle were ill-defined even in Europe, where the terrain was more favorable.

In the Civil War battles there were often openings for large reserve masses of cavalry to intervene, but they were rarely taken. At Gaines's Mill the Union cavalry was sent in too weak; at Gettysburg almost all the Confederate cavalry was elsewhere. In many other battles, too, there was inadequate attention paid to this arm. It did not deliver what it might have delivered on the battlefield, regardless of what it achieved in scouting or raiding.

**Artillery** was the real 'heavy weapon' of these battles, with enormous killing power at close range and deterrent power at long range. If used *en masse* at the right point, it could control the action. Unfortunately it took a long time for the armies to realize this, and although there were some early examples of massed batteries (eg Malvern Hill, Second Manassas), the organizational structures of North and South were slow to adjust to the concept. In the Western theater they never really adjusted to it at all. The result was that for most of the war the artillery was a local weapon, used in piecemeal and not exploited as a 'massed reserve'. If it was used *en masse* at all, it was normally in a position chosen before the battle began.

Artillery was certainly more effective in the Civil War on the defensive than on the offensive. Creative maneuvers to bring it up in support of an attack were beyond the scope of most generals. In many cases the preparatory fire for an assault was fired at too long range, or not for long enough, to be effective (eg US guns at Antietam and Fredericksburg, CS at Gettysburg).

**Defense in Depth** was the logical result of keeping reserves behind a fighting line - often more accidental than planned, although there were exceptions (*eg* Jackson at Fredericksburg, many of Johnston's positions before Atlanta). Obviously, the deeper the defenses at the point attacked, the more chance there was of successful resistance - provided the men were not packed together so closely they got in each other's way. At Chattanooga the rearmost Confederate lines were prevented from firing by the withdrawal of the front lines, leading to a rout by everyone.

The density needed for defense varied with terrain, fortification, and the weight of attack:-

| Place | Average Men Per Mile | Comments |
| --- | --- | --- |
| Petersburg '64-5 (CS) | 1,000 | Well fortified, rarely seriously attacked. |
| Atlanta campaign '64 (CS) | 1,000-2,000 | Well fortified. Usually retired to new position if strongly attacked. |
| Atlanta campaign '64 (US) | 3,000-4,000 | Well fortified. Usually retired to new position if strongly attacked. |
| Antietam '62 (CS) | 8,000 | Unfortified open fields. The line almost broke. |
| Fredericksburg '62 (CS) | 16,000 | Lightly fortified. Proof against all attack. |
| Shiloh '62 (US) | 20,000 | Unfortified but in strong terrain. Mauled but not broken by attack. |
| Gettysburg '63 (US) | 26,000 | Light fortification in strong terrain. Proof against attack. |

**Depth in Attack** was usually laid on too thick in Civil War battles: a mass of men would assault on a narrow front and become mixed together in confusion (*eg* US at Second Manassas had 50,000 men per mile): CS in Pickett's charge at Gettysburg had 15,000 in half a mile). More effective tactics would have been to feed in men more gradually.

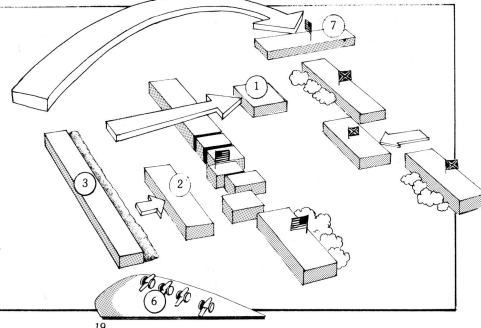

**Counter-Attacks** were potentially the most effective use of reserves, especially if they could hit the enemy at the moment of maximum exhaustion and demoralization after his own attack had failed.

The main problems with counter-attacks were -

*Timing:* hitting the enemy after he has made his move but before he has consolidated it.

*Direction:* hitting him where he's weak

*The Passage of Lines:* It is important to bring the reserves through the troops who are already fighting without disorganizing either. Often very difficult in the tumult of battle!

**The Use of Reserves** included the following roles:-

1) To *counter-attack* the enemy, if he seemed vulnerable.

2) To *reinforce* one's own line, if it was under pressure.

3) To make a *retrenchment* in rear of one's line, if it was crumbling (= defense in depth)

4) To *wait* in reserve, to see what happened next

5) To make a *rearguard stand* against a very victorious enemy

6) To create a *massed battery* of artillery to dominate ground of special importance

7) To make a *wide flanking maneuver* with any or all arms - but best done with cavalry.

# THE PURSUIT PHASE

When a general wins his battle he will be faced with the problem of what to do next. Most of the pressures will be in the direction of doing nothing, resting and regrouping - even though this will allow most of the beaten enemy to escape and fight another day.

Few Civil War battles ended with a crushing pursuit which might have converted an 'ordinary victory' into a 'decisive rout'

of the opponent. Whether because the winning side was exhausted, or lacked good information, or had no pursuit forces at hand, the loser usually managed to slip away before his defeated units could be rounded up. An army fleeing from danger naturally moved faster than an army moving through a broken battlefield into the uncertainties and redoubled efforts which lay beyond.

**The Commander** needs maximum energy for pursuit at the moment it is psychologically most difficult for him to raise it - *ie* at the end of a hard but successful day's battle. The harder the fighting has been, the more he will imagine the enemy is strong. The more successful he has been, the more he will be tempted to sit back and congratulate himself. He will require enormous powers of imagination and insight to realize just how bad things must be looking 'on the other side of the hill' or to remember that 'There is only one thing worse than winning a battle, and that is losing one'.

The fact of having fought will also have distracted the commander from the task of collecting intelligence. His cavalry screen may have been engaged in exciting skirmishes instead of careful observations; his signal stations may have been too preoccupied sending urgent orders to be attentive to what the enemy is doing. A hundred pressing requests may interfere with the key command responsibility of (a) identifying changes in the enemy posture, as a stout defense is replaced by a rearguard playing for time, and (b) deciding who must press home the pursuit, and with what troops in which direction. All this is enormously difficult to get right in most eras of military history, and in the Civil War it seems to have been more difficult than ever.

**Local Truces** were often arranged between soldiers who had been fighting hard, giving them an opportunity to succor the wounded and bury the dead. 'Live and let live' was only a natural human response to the terrifying ordeal of combat, especially when the soldiers of each side had discovered that the battle lines were too strong to break. What was the use of fighting on? Peaceful regrouping and even friendly conversations between opposing picket lines seemed to be a more sensible end to a day's battle than a frenzied pursuit and a new battle in the obscurity of dusk.

**The Effect of Battle** was to drive men to earth and disorganize units. Soldiers would be reluctant to abandon positions they had painfully dug for themselves under enemy fire, and many would be absent from the roll call:- casualties, skulkers, those honourably helping the wounded and those dishonorably stripping the dead. Ammunition would have been used up and rifles fouled with burned powder. Water might well be lacking to assuage men dehydrated by their exertions. Food would often all have been consumed in the march to contact, or to keep the soldiers active during the firefight. Essential items of clothing or cooking utensils would have been cast aside in

thrilling 'packs down' charges. Rifles would have been cast aside in terror or rendered useless by faulty loading. Veterans might have decided that they had done their duty and would do no more today, while greenhorns might be excitedly re-living their moment of glory, oblivious to the continuing demands of their officers. Those officers themselves might be squabbling about real or imagined errors in the way the battle had been fought, or simply scouring the rear areas for missing men and supplies. Gun teams might be immobilized for want of horses. Only the most energetic leadership could get such an army on the road again within a few hours of the end of a battle.

*Tired troops halted in a ragged firing line.*

*Wounded and stragglers stream to the rear.*

**Special Artists** and journalists were to be found quite close to the front lines on both sides. The artists' rapid on-the-spot sketches were rushed back to their city newspapers to be worked-up by wood block specialists into the final image to be printed.

Here Alfred Waud draws the final stage of the action for "Harper's Weekly". He covered every major engagement of the Army of the Potomac, but kept his British passport handy - 'just in case'.

**The Timing** of most Civil War pursuit operations shows the seriousness of the problem. After Gettysburg the first Union moves to follow up were made some twelve hours after the fighting ended, and the two infantry bodies started in motion only after 36 hours. At the end of Chickamauga there was the same delay before the Confederate pursuit, which General D H Hill called 'the great blunder of all' and Nathan B Forrest lamented as "every hour was worth a thousand men". After Second Manassas there was also a 24 hour delay in pursuing the routed Northern troops, and after Chattanooga there was an overnight pause while the victorious Union commanders realized that their opponent was on the run.

The more offensively-minded commanders, such as US Grant and John B Hood, always made a point of emphasising the need to capture trophies from the enemy - flags, guns, baggage and prisoners. They realized that these were the only genuine indicator that the enemy had been seriously damaged by battle. If he simply lost men killed or wounded it did not necessarily mean that he had been routed. Nevertheless even Hood and Grant found it easier to pick up a few trophies on the battlefield itself than to win them in large numbers by successful, annihilating pursuits.

**The Rearguard** of a defeated army had three functions. One was simply to conceal the army's discomfiture from the enemy and therefore forestall his thought of starting a pursuit. Secondly the rearguard had to fight out the final act in a battle while the main body broke clean away - eg Thomas at Chickamauga prevented the Confederate from moving into the pursuit by his obstinate resistance towards nightfall. Finally, if the worst came to the worst a rearguard could delay a pursuit after it had advanced beyond the battlefield - eg Cleburne made a stand on the Ringgold Road some time after the Chattanooga battle had finished.

**The Vulnerability** of an army in flight cannot be over-stated. Separated from their units, many soldiers lose all military effectiveness and sometimes lose the army altogether. The temptation to loot friendly baggage trains is great (eg the Confederates after Chattanooga), and the desperate measures taken by officers and battle-police to stop the rout lead to summary punishments and ill-feeling. Only the most solid and steadfast units - or the units which have not been in action - maintain their organization and fighting spirit. The rest melt away, haunted by irrational fears of a rapid enemy advance or simply by the desire to lie down and sleep.

In these circumstances it is essential that a retreating army has a clear and open road ahead of it. If its way is blocked by a river or a traffic jam in a defile, then it will offer an almost entirely helpless target to an enterprising enemy pursuit.

*Enemy rearguard stands firm.*

*Unseen, the broken enemy army is in full retreat towards the river.*

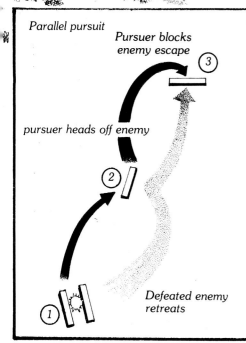

*Parallel pursuit*

*Pursuer blocks enemy escape*

③

*pursuer heads off enemy*

②

①

*Defeated enemy retreats*

## THEORY OF PURSUIT

The obvious way to launch a pursuit was simply to follow in the enemy's footsteps, picking up his stragglers and jostling his rearguard as much as possible. Often there was no alternative to this, when movements were channeled by the layout of roads and terrain. A more decisive means of pursuit, however, lay in advancing parallel to the retreating enemy and trying to outmarch him to his objective. If you could set up a road block ahead of him, and then surround him, you had a good chance of capturing his entire army. This is what Grant and Sheridan managed to do in the Appomattox campaign. A third option was to leave a 'Golden Bridge' open for the enemy's escape, and not to harrass him at all. This made sense if you thought he was too strong, or if he might spread dissension when he got back to friendly territory - but usually in the Civil War (eg for McClellan after Antietam) it spelled a lost opportunity.

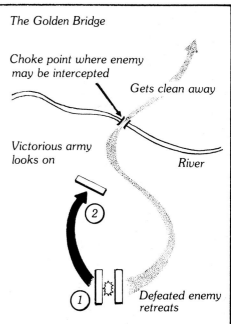

*The Golden Bridge*

*Choke point where enemy may be intercepted*

*Gets clean away*

*Victorious army looks on*

*River*

②

①

*Defeated enemy retreats*

# PART THREE : CORPS AND DIVISION COMMAND
## THE LEVELS OF COMMAND

Civil War armies were complex **organizations,** and much **depended on their** "middle management" - the corps and division commanders who were responsible for translating the army commander's intentions into movements on the ground. It was at these levels of command that we find the overall direction of battles taking place: below them (*ie* among the brigade and regimental commanders) came the realm of details and minor tactics.

Corps and division commanders often enjoyed considerable independence, operating at a distance from army headquarters and even fighting separate battles, *eg* during Chancellorsville Early was left to hold the Confederate rear near Fredericksburg with one division. In 1864 this same officer was sent raiding towards Washington with a detached corps.

**A Corps Commander** was a very senior and trusted general, eligible to command a whole army if vacancies fell due - a circumstance which often led to fierce rivalries between contenders. A corps sometimes consisted of all arms, although more normally it was either infantry or cavalry plus artillery in each case. This sometimes left the infantry corps short of cavalry for local scouting and support duties.

Corps HQ in battle would usually be safely behind the fighting, with elaborate administrative and signalling arrangements. The corps commander would not usually be able to see a very large proportion of his troops, and would have to guess what they were doing on the basis of noises and signals. He would not be involved in the details of battle, but would order the general movements of each division and his artillery reserve.

Rank : Lieutenant General/Major General

**The Army Commander**
Rank : General/Lieutenant General/Major General

**A Divison Commander** was usually on his way to the top, but had not yet quite broken into the charmed circle of high command. He would have a more personal detailed knowledge of the men under his command, and his staff would be less bureaucratic than that of the corps commander. A division would often contain the same brigades for a long period of time, making it possible for each one to imprint its own character upon the division as a whole.

In battle the division commander would be quite near the firing line, but would normally have to keep free enough to manage a reserve of one or more of his brigades. He would often be responsible for the tactical details of attack or **defense,** although he might also leave this to his brigade commanders.

Rank : Major General/Brigadier General

**A Brigade Commander** had to be a real 'soldier's soldier', leading his men from the front and becoming personally involved in every battle. The brigade was the basic tactical unit, especially since 'march losses' soon reduced each regiment to a third or a quarter of its official size (*ie* to an average of 400 instead of 1,050), leaving it too small to achieve very much on its own. Each regiment was therefore thrown closely together with the others in the brigade, making close-knit military 'family' presided over by the brigade commander. All the regiments often came from the same area, and there was trouble when outsiders were brought in to make up for losses.
Rank : Brigadier General/Colonel

**A Regimental Commander** was responsible for only a very small part of any battlefield - maybe only 50-100 yards front. Within that area he would have to keep his ten companies in line, and urge them to do their duty. He would seldom have to take tactical decisions, but would often have to set an example and display high qualities of leadership and man-management. Sometimes he would have the benefit of a horse to ride - sometimes not. But he would always have to use his voice and his energy to get things done. Regimental commanders often had pre-war military experience or high social status, whereas this was not generally true of the more junior levels of command (except perhaps in favored branches like the staff, or branches where promotion was slow, such as the artillery).
Rank: Colonel Lieutenant-Colonel/Major

**A Company Commander** in theory had two or three commissioned officers plus 8-10 non-commissioned officers to support him. In practice the companies often shrank so small that there were barely one commissioned and three or four non-commissioned officers to command, say, 40 men. The company commander would march on foot in the infantry, and share almost all the discomforts and dangers of the rank and file.
Rank : Captain/Lieutenant/Second Lieutenant/Sergeant

**Recruits** were mostly 3-year volunteers, with some 3-month volunteers in the initial campaigns and maybe 40,000 regulars altogether. Both sides resorted to conscription eventually, but conscripts always remained a small minority overall. The Union (with a population of 22 m) enlisted some 3 m in total, while the Confederacy (with a white population of 5.5 m) enlisted 1.2 m, to which must be added the extensive rear echelon use of black slave labor. In the 'average' volunteer infantry regiment the fate of the men might be as follows:-

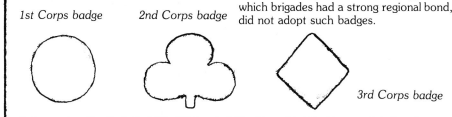

| | Union | Confederate |
|---|---|---|
| Average strength on mobilisation | 1,050 | 1,050 |
| Reinforcements joining later | 250 | 500 |
| Hence total strength in war | 1,300 | 1,550 |
| Wounded in battle (includes walking wounded) | 150 | 365 |
| Died of disease in friendly hands | 130 | 300 |
| Deserted and not recaptured | 120 | 200 |
| Deserted and recaptured | 30 | 60 |
| Died in or as result of battle | 32 | 90 |
| Died while in enemy hands (all causes) | 20 | 50 |
| Died by accident, murder, suicide etc (other than in battle) | 3 | ? |
| Hence total definitively lost to the unit | 305 (+) | 640 (+) |

We must conclude that despite the greater strength of each Confederate infantry regiment than its Union counterpart, life there was more exciting, more active and more dangerous. They were, after all, heavily outnumbered throughout the war and were therefore thrown into battle more often. Note that on both sides many of those who were not 'definitively lost to the unit' managed to get by without actually serving with the unit in the front line, while many of those who died, from whatever cause, had successfully completed many months of loyal service at the sharp end. One Confederate Major who was killed in 1864 had fought in no less than 107 engagements.

## UNIT IDENTIFICATION BADGES

In March 1863 Hooker issued a circular advocating the adoption of unit badges, to aid "... ready recognition of corps and divisions of this army and to prevent injustice by reports of straggling and misconduct through mistakes as to their organizations."

A year earlier General Phil Kearney's division had worn pieces of red blanket material on their hats as a unit insignia. By the end of the war most Union soldiers were wearing hat badges which showed their corps and division. This may have helped with the chronic problem of straggling, and certainly strengthened the *esprit de corps* of Union formations. The Confederate army, in which brigades had a strong regional bond, did not adopt such badges.

*1st Corps badge*          *2nd Corps badge*

*3rd Corps badge*

*Scheme- 1st Div Red, 2nd Div White, 3rd Div Blue, 4th Div Orange, 5th Div Green*

**Organization** varied considerably at different times and places, especially in the chaotic early months of the war, when many strange 'legions' and independent companies sprang up. Standardization was fairly complete by the end of the war, with 10 companies per regiment of infantry volunteers and Confederate cavalry; 12 companies/troops per regiment of Union artillery and cavalry; 2 battalions each of 8 companies per regiment of Union regular infantry. Brigades, however, tended to have more regiments at the end than at the start of the war, but each regiment was far smaller - eg at First Manassas the average was 3.9 regiments per brigade; at Cold Harbor it was nearer 5.5 overall, with particularly numerous regiments in Union brigades. An extreme was Colonel McKeen's 1st Brigade of 1st Division, II Corps. It included:-

- 19th Maine
- 15th Massachusetts
- 19th Massachusetts
- 20th Massachusetts
- 1st Massachusetts Sharpshooter Company
- 7th Michigan
- 42nd New York
- 59th New York
- 82nd New York (one batallion only)
- 184th Pennsylvania
- 36th Wisconsin

The Confederates managed to make do with fewer regiments per brigade, with greater unity of local origin. Not unusual was Daniel's Brigade of Rode's division, also at Cold Harbor:-

- 32nd North Carolina
- 43rd North Carolina
- 45th North Carolina
- 53rd North Carolina
- 2nd North Carolina Battalion

*Union and Confederate westerners*

*Union Negro infantryman*

*Irish Brigade member*

*Confederate Indian soldier*

**The Combattants** came in all shapes and sizes! There were Indian regiments in the Western theatre and self-styled Scottish Highlanders in New York. Almost 200,000 blacks joined the Union army, as well as some 750,000 foreigners (of which 60% were either German or Irish). On both sides, especially, there was a distinction drawn between the 'Westerners' and the 'Easterners'. Westerners were supposed to be big-boned, lanky farmhands with no use for formalism or 'European manners'. Easterners were supposed to be (in the North) quick-witted city dwellers or (in the South) etiquette-conscious gentlefolk. In reality none of these stereotypes was really firmly based - but there was a grain of truth in all of them.

# COMING INTO ACTION

**Corps and Division Commanders** followed a routine for coming into action which was similar to that of the army commander, but proportionately smaller in scale. First the troops march to the area where the enemy is thought to be; then there is a reconnaissance phase; then orders are issued for attack or **defense**. The battle starts with preparatory fire from infantry skirmishers and artillery, with attacks moving in centrally or around a flank. As the clash of arms subsides the commander must decide whether a pursuit is possible or whether reserves are needed for a rearguard stand.

At this level of command, however, there are more details to be supervised than at the army commander's more lofty position. The corps and division commanders must establish liaison with other friendly troops who may be operating on the flanks or held behind in reserve. Precise positions must be allocated for batteries, infantry brigades and breastworks. In other words, the battle must be 'fought' as well as 'managed'.

**The Zone of Danger** was determined by the range of weapons: not by their theoretical maximum range but by their effective battle range, *ie* the range at which troops felt it was worthwhile to open fire. Exact figures have no meaning when it comes to determining effective battle range, since it was a subjective decision on the part of individual soldiers. Nevertheless we might offer the following as a rough guide:-

| Weapon | Theoretical Maximum Range (in yards) | Effective Battle Range (in yards) |
|---|---|---|
| Rifled Cannon, Heavy | 3,000 | 2,000 |
| Rifled Cannon, Light | 1,800 | 1,800 |
| Smoothbore Cannon | 1,600 | 800 |
| Sniper Rifle | 1,700 | 600 |
| Enfield/Springfield Rifle Musket | 1,000 | 200 |
| Older Rifles | 400 | 100 |
| Smoothbore Musket | 200 | 50 |
| Breechloading Rifles/Carbines | 800 | 125 |
| Pistols | 100 | 10 |

Troops would happily stand in the open beyond the effective range of smoothbore cannon, or under cover beyond the effective range of rifle muskets. These two were the mainstay weapons of the Civil War armies: the longer-ranged sniper rifles and rifled cannon were more specialised and less widespread. Sniper rifles in particular were in very short supply, making up perhaps 0.1% of each army's infantry armament. Within the danger zone of rifle muskets the troops felt themselves to be in 'close combat' with the enemy, and it was hard for higher commanders to get them to perform maneuvers of any complexity. Usually the two lines stood firing at each other until one or the other ran out of ammunition, or energy, or courage.

**Skirmish Fire** was the alternative to a stand-up firefight between two formed lines at close range. In skirmish fire a relatively small number of troops (one or two companies per regiment) would fan out and take cover individually at a safely long range from the enemy. They would keep up a harrassing fire, but not attempt to attack. This could go on for hours, especially if the skirmish line was relieved from time to time from the main body of its supports. The skirmishers would be very difficult for the enemy to hit, yet their fire would be a considerable nuisance even if it did not actually strike many men.

Skirmishing of this type could be used to keep the enemy in play while a major attack was being assembled, or to screen a move to flank or rear. In the offensive skirmishers could probe forward to find weak points in the enemy's line. At the end of combat the skirmish screen turned into the army's line of infantry pickets for routine security. They therefore had many uses and were almost always deployed ahead of the main fighting positions of Civil War armies.

**Snipers** were simply 'skirmishers who could shoot straight'. Unlike the majority of skirmishers they could expect a high proporition of their shots to fall near the enemy, even at long ranges. A few snipers firing for a long period could therefore make a battery position untenable, or force a fighting line to take cover. They could even sometimes pick off officers, such as the unfortunate General Sedgwick in the Wilderness battle. Their weapons were highly specialised and delicate, however, and unsuitable for the rough and tumble of close action.

**The Concept of Defense** in the Civil War was quite straightforward: if the enemy pushed through your outpost lines of pickets he was to be stopped by a main line of resistance placed on a strong feature - a stone wall, a railroad embankment or specially built fortifications. Ideally there would be several supporting lines stepped up a hill overlooking the main line, so all the fire could be brought to bear together. The support lines would in any case give depth and provide a reserve, even if they did not have the elevation to contribute in this way. Even if the attacker captured the main line of defense, therefore, the battle would not be over. He would have to start all over again, giving the defender a chance to rally his reserves or launch a counter-attack.

The principle of cross-fire or flanking fire was important to defensive layouts, and engineer officers skilled in the science of geometry were often consulted when a line was being traced. Their aim would be to make the most of the terrain contours to ensure that an attack on any one part of the position could be taken in flank from another part.

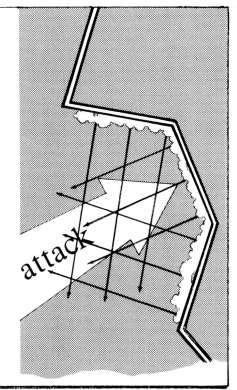

**The Fireplan** of a Civil War defense would not usually be very clearly laid down, but in essence it would amount to four distinct phases:

1) The long-ranged rifled cannon try to prevent the enemy's artillery from establishing itself within effective battle range. There is a counter-battery duel for artillery supremacy.

2) If the defender wins the counter-battery duel he has no problem in using his main artillery mass (mostly smoothbores) against attacking infantry. If he loses the duel, however, he will have to pull back his guns into cover and bring them into action again only when the attacking infantry is close.

3) Skirmishers also keep up a harassing fire as the enemy attack comes close, although they will probably be forced to pull back hastily and may not have a chance to deliver many shots.

4) Finally the main defensive line will be ordered to hold its fire until the attack is very close indeed, when a devastating volley can be delivered, folowed by either fire at will or, still more damaging, a counter-charge. Only very good troops could get all this right, however, and many Civil War regiments simply blazed away as soon as the enemy came within effective battle range.

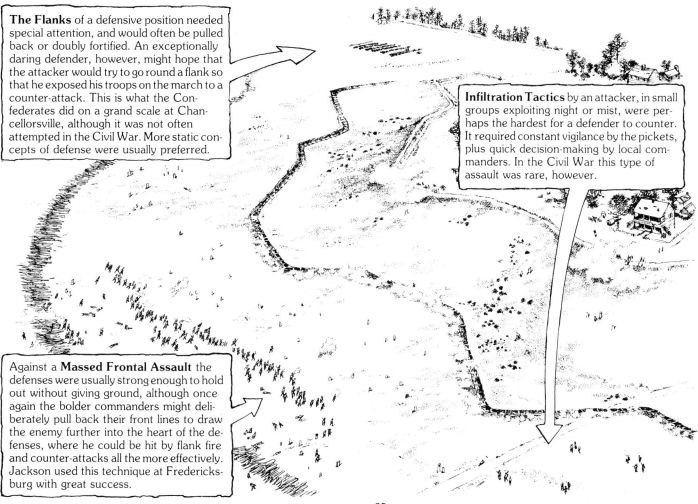

**The Flanks** of a defensive position needed special attention, and would often be pulled back or doubly fortified. An exceptionally daring defender, however, might hope that the attacker would try to go round a flank so that he exposed his troops on the march to a counter-attack. This is what the Confederates did on a grand scale at Chancellorsville, although it was not often attempted in the Civil War. More static concepts of defense were usually preferred.

**Infiltration Tactics** by an attacker, in small groups exploiting night or mist, were perhaps the hardest for a defender to counter. It required constant vigilance by the pickets, plus quick decision-making by local commanders. In the Civil War this type of assault was rare, however.

Against a **Massed Frontal Assault** the defenses were usually strong enough to hold out without giving ground, although once again the bolder commanders might deliberately pull back their front lines to draw the enemy further into the heart of the defenses, where he could be hit by flank fire and counter-attacks all the more effectively. Jackson used this technique at Fredericksburg with great success.

# THE PLACE OF ARTILLERY

Artillery was an auxiliary arm in the Civil War. It could not win battles on its own without the help of infantry or cavalry. Yet it was nevertheless an essential auxiliary which greatly enhanced the power of a force, provided it was used correctly. Civil War commanders usually made sure it was used large numbers of guns available in their battles, even though in certain special circumstances they might reduce their artillery parks (eg Grant sent home 120 guns for his campaign in the difficult terrain of the Wilderness: Sherman had only one gun per 1,000 men for his unconventional march to the sea). The normal ratio was 2 - 4 guns per 1,000 men, although Lee occasionally reached 8 - 10 in his undermanned Army of Northern Virginia.

The correct use of artillery was in mass at medium ranges and with crossed fire. If, say, 100 guns could be organized in front of a defensive position, in order to cover a frontage of a thousand yards, it would make the enemy's attacks far more difficult than if he had to face musketry alone.

**Long Range Fire** was the speciality of the new rifled cannons which were coming into service in the 1860s, allowing accuracy at a mile range which had previously been unobtainable. These weapons suffered several disadvantages, however, so they were not ideally suited to meet all the requirements of artillery in general. Their projectiles were relatively lightweight, which gave them low explosive power, and especially on the Confederate side the shells were very unreliable. Since rifled artillery was still in its infancy there were also rather too many accidental barrel bursts for the crews' peace of mind. It was to be only in the Franco Prussian War of 1870 that the full potential of rifled cannon came to be realized.

Notable feats of long range accuracy were nevertheless performed with the rifles, for example the killing of the Confederate General 'Bishop' Polk on the Kenesaw line (although this turned out to be purely

*Sighting a rifled gun*

accidental rather than deliberate assassination). And at both Fredericksburg and Antietam the Union artillery was able to achieve fire superiority over the Confederate guns at over a mile range. This didn't win the battles for the North, however, since the Southern artillery could withdraw under cover until needed to repel infantry attacks at close range.

Supporting an attack by long range fire was rarely very effective in the Civil War, since the trajectory was too flat and the attackers themselves tended to mask the target from their own gunners. Another problem with such direct fire was that the enemy could gain protection simply by sheltering behind cover. There was little high angle indirect fire to seek him out, although short range mortars were used during the various sieges, especially at Petersburg. Even then the techniques of fire control were rudimentary.

---

## ORGANISATION

*4 Gun battery at regulation spacing. Guns could be deployed much closer than shown if necessary. Horse teams may be unhitched and moved into cover for long engagements.*

*50 yards*

At the start of the war batteries were attached to each brigade of infantry, and sometimes even to individual regiments. As experience in the massing of fire was gained, however, the batteries came to be grouped in battalions (CSA) or brigades (USA) under their own commanders, independently of the infantry. This allowed the full firepower to be co-ordinated effectively according to the particular requirements of the arm.

Each battery had three or, more usually, (especially in the Confederate army) two sections, each of two guns. Ideally there would be a total of 25 men per gun in the battery, of which 9 would directly serve the gun in battle. In practice, however, the total men per gun was usually 15-20. Each gun had a limber and two caissons, each with six horses, which with supporting vehicles (forge and supply wagons) might make a battery a sizeable target. 4 guns, 15 vehicles, 90 men, 90 horses might be seen as a 'typical' battery organization.

In theory a limber for the 'Napoleon' carried 32 rounds and a caisson carried 96 rounds, making 224 rounds per gun carried in the battery, mostly shells and solid shot. In practice batteries seldom had that much ammunition available, and might need replenishment from central reserve parks after firing a hundred or so shots per gun - which in itself was a high average for a battle. At Gettysburg the Army of the Potomac fired about that many, but Gettysburg was an especially hard-fought affair. On that occasion a total of 270 rounds per gun were available within the army, as a result of the provision of special additional reserve parks. On the Confederate side each gun had only about 230 rounds to last it through the entire campaign.

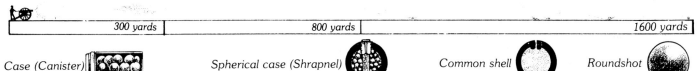

| Case (Canister) | Spherical case (Shrapnel) | Common shell | Roundshot |

**The Napoleon Twelve Pounder** was the 'classic' artillery weapon of the Civil War - a handy maid of all work which was found to give the most useful overall service. It was a smoothbore, lacking the range of the unpredictable rifled guns, but more than making up for this by ease of operation and the power of its blasts.

Its ammunition could be (1) simple solid shot for battering or grazing fire;

(2) 'spherical case' or 'shrapnel' shell consisting of a hollow sphere filled with musket balls and a charge which could be **fuzed** to burst in the air over an enemy, scattering the contents over him; (3) 'common' shell composed of a hollow sphere filled with powder, time-fuzed to burst on the ground on arrival at the enemy; (4) Grape and canister in various sizes - *ie* a tin full of round balls of varying weights, to be used as an

anti-personnel weapon on the scatter-gun principle. The propellant charge was $2\frac{1}{2}$ lbs of black powder, which made a numbing crash when detonated.

Solid shot had the longest range and shrapnel had a 500 yard minimum range. Grape and canister were for short range emergencies only, especially 200 yards or less, although some heavy versions could reach out to 800 yards.

**The Casualties** inflicted by artillery have often been minimized by historians, and it is true that shells and shrapnel rounds were more damaging to the enemy's morale than to his soldiers (due to the faulty fuzes and the problem of setting the rage accurately. etc). The booming blasts of a Napoleon could be very demoralising indeed to an attacker (and heartening to friendly forces) even without scoring many hits. In Grant's campaign in the spring of 1864 the Union casualty statistics show that Confederate roundshot and shell caused only 6% of his losses, which looks an almost trivial total, slightly less than the 7% caused by accidents or self-inflicted wounds.

Yet in some other battles the killing power of the guns was enormous. At Malvern Hill the Union artillery inflicted a good half of the Confederate loss, and at Fredericksburg at least twenty per cent of the Northern casualties were caused by Lee's gunners. A great deal depended on the terrain and the way the guns were sited.

Enemy batteries could be silenced by counter-battery fire in anything from a few minutes to $1\frac{1}{2}$ hours or so. It didn't usually take more than 10% losses to persuade a battery to pull out, although sometimes they did admittedly fight on until they had suffered 30%, 40% or even (on one occasion) 60% casualties.

**Close Range Fire** was the really damaging way to use artillery against infantry, in both attack and defense. It was naturally easier for this to happen in defense since the enemy infantry would come to the guns, whereas in the attack the guns would have to go to the enemy infantry. Hence the power of Civil War artillery was usually a factor which strengthened a defense.

The effective movement of artillery to support an attack at close range from the defender's position was a skill which was rarely exhibited in the Civil War. There were

few 'artillery charges' of the kind seen occasionally in Napoleonic times. Why was this? Probably the main reason was a matter of doctrine: the artillery charge was a concept associated too closely with the excessive subordination to the infantry which had reduced the effectiveness of gun-power early in the war. The gunners wanted independence! The artillery charge was also difficult because of terrain obstacles and the need for good timing, and it was dangerous in the face of strong enemy fire unless it could be executed very slickly and

decisively. At Gettysburg the Confederate artillery commander, General Alexander, thought it was safe to try an artillery charge against Sickles' advanced troops in the Peach Orchard only after they had started to withdraw.

Yet a few artillerists on both sides did make a habit of running their guns close to the enemy and slugging it out eyeball-to-eyeball. Chew and the bespectacled Pelham, of the Confederate horse artillery, were especially famous for this, although they were only able ever to do it on a small scale.

# THE CONCEPT OF ATTACK

The defense enjoyed many advantages in the Civil War, and attackers suffered many costly failures. Nevertheless it remained true throughout the war that you were forced to make an assault, sooner or later, if you wanted to maintain your forward progress against the enemy. Several generals developed 'flanking' methods in the attempt to avoid the need for assaults; but even they from time to time were forced to take the bull by the horns. Unfortunately there was a relative lack of specialist training for the assault, which was a particularly difficult operation. **This further strengthened the advantages of the defender, led to still more 'slaughter pens' and the eventual discrediting of the idea of assault itself.**

### Artillery Support

Despite the general failure to bring guns close to the enemy to support attacks, there was agreement that it was useful to prepare an attack by an artillery bombardment. Even if it could not kill many of the defender's soldiers, it could at least chase off his artillery and create a useful advantage of *morale*. But the attacking infantry commander would need to act in close concert with the artillery commander to agree timings and positions for the barrage.

**Surprise** was another factor which a wise attacker would hope to employ. Hit the enemy from a direction he did not expect, preferably on flank or rear; hit him at a time when he was off guard, perhaps at dawn or dusk; hit him under the cover of night or mist, or by impersonating one of his own units. All of these techniques were used at different times, and enjoyed a better than average record of success; yet we may wonder whether they were used as often or as systematically as they might have been.

Much depended on the personality in command. Boldly maneuvering corps commanders (*eg* Jackson) could bewilder the enemy by their rapid movements, or shrewd divisional commanders (*eg* Griffin) could set up aggressive and effective dawn raids. A Hood or an Upton could win good successes with well-orchestrated brigade attacks. But these men were few and far between. The predominant concept of offensive operations was more formal and more predictable. It depended on mass rather than surprise, and on cumbersome successions of lines rather than lightly-maneuvering small units. This really represented a lost opportunity in tactics, and more than one Confederate soldier at Petersburg, for example, expressed astonishment that the Union did not try more subtle infiltration attacks than they actually did, since in many places the defensive lines were actually a lot less strong than they looked.

---

**Assault Drills** were usually based on the idea of waves of infantry striking the enemy one after another at a short selected sector of his line. The aim was to maintain momentum by replacing the first line by the second as soon as it faltered, and so on. The attack could be preceded by a 'bow wave' of skirmishers extending beyond the flanks, and it might be flanked by troops advancing in column ready to face outwards to meet any threat from that direction. Sometimes each assaulting regiment would be formed in line (*ie* making it an attack by a column of lines) and sometimes in column (making a column of columns). It scarcely mattered which, since the overall result was to place a milling mass of men in close contact with the enemy's position.

The distance between lines was very variable. In theory it was intended to be at least 200 yards and sometimes as much as 800, to avoid mixing the second line too closely in the first line's battle until it was called forward to help. In practice, however, the pressures of combat led commanders to close this distance to 150 yards, 75 yards or even less. Obviously if the first line halted when it bumped the enemy but the second line did not halt, not many minutes would elapse before the two merged together into one.

In Upton's justly famous attack on the 'Angle' at Spotsylvania a refinement was added in that the first line was intended to break off to right and left as soon as it entered the enemy position, leaving the second line to continue the fight in greater depth, supported by the third line, leaving the fourth line 200 yards short as an ultimate reserve. This concept showed a quite modern understanding of the need to keep momentum even after the first enemy line had been carried, although in practice much of the sophistication was swept away and the troops all entered the enemy lines in one formless mob.

**Reinforcing Success** rather than failure is a classic military principle, but it was 'easier said than done' in the circumstances of major Civil War infantry attacks. The large masses of men were unweildy and slow to maneuver if there was a lasy-minute change of plan. It was usually difficult for a corps or division commander to see exactly what was going on unless he moved close to the firing - and if he did that he risked losing touch with 'the big picture'. Finally there was a certain inertia inevitably produced by combat itself. Once a regiment had captured one enemy position it would be reluctant to move on against another; once it had gone to ground it would want to stay there.

*Upton's divisional attack at Spotsylvania*

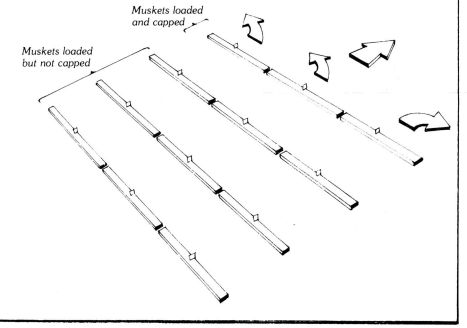

Muskets loaded and capped

Muskets loaded but not capped

**The Fog of War** could be the result of many factors - wooded terrain or battle-smoke obscuring the view; leaders in the front line failing to get back timely messages to the rear; misunderstanding of the messages which did get through. Troops making an approach march through broken ground quite often lost their way and attacked the enemy in a different place than intended (**eg** Newton's attack at Kenesaw Mountain), or found that they couldn't make contact with troops they were supposed to be supporting (**eg** several of the Confederate units lost each other at the battle of Seven Pines). Once again, all this tended to work against the attacker who had to keep moving, rather than against the defender who was relatively static.

Also working against a commander's intention to maintain momentum was the natural hesitation of subordinates caught between an impatient higher order to attack, and daunting local knowledge that the enemy's position was very strong. At Nashville one brigadier complained to General Thomas' courier that a proposed attack would be "Suicide, sir, perfect suicide" - nevertheless the attack did succeed perfectly despite these gloomy predictions.

**The Sequence of an Attack** might be as follows:-

1) Artillery and skirmisher preparation until fire superiority gained (if that is possible) - 30-120 minutes?

2) Assault forces move forward, preferably preceded by a feint attack at a different spot (feint 30 minutes before main attack) - Main attack advances at walk (90 or 110 paces per minute, say 50 yards in normally rough country) until within 1-200 yards of enemy.

3) First line breaks into a charge at 1-200 **yards from enemy, hoping to overrun his** works firing only one volley on the way, at 20 yards (165-200 paces per minute, say 100 yards per minute, losing close order formation).

4) If successful, first line regroups on target, second line passes through and repeats the process against the next enemy position (allow 15-30 minutes for the second attack to be **organized**).

If unsuccessful, first line goes to ground and fires off most of its ammunition, then second line passes through to the assault (allow 45-120 minutes for the firefight, 15-30 for the assault).

5) Keep doing this for as long as it takes. If you can't make progress, dig in where you are.

**Going to Ground** near the enemy is the natural reaction of troops who (rightly or wrongly) don't think they can overrun him. The range may be anything from 200 to 10 yards from the enemy when this happens, but when it does happen it means that this particular attack has run into trouble. Maybe its officers will be able to get it moving forward again, or maybe they won't. Maybe it will be able to chase off the enemy by firepower after all, without needing that final assault. More likely it won't.

When the main armies of the two sides took the field in 1862 there was plenty of willingness to push on for the final assault, and hence the chances of success were better than even (even though losses were high). Battles were often quite fluid, with attacks and counter-attacks following each other in regular order. By 1864, however, there were too many veterans in the ranks who had been through the fire too often. A great reluctance to assault earthworks set in, and assault orders were frequently 'inter-preted' to mean little more than 'advance forward as skirmishers a little way, then go to ground at a safe distance from the enemy and exchange harmless pot-shots with him'. At Gettysburg something like 1-200 rounds were fired for each casualty inflicted, which indicates some pretty close, hard fighting. In Sherman's battles between Chattanooga and Atlanta the figure was nearer 1,000 rounds per casualty, which indicates a different attitude.

# THE PASSAGE OF LINES

Perhaps the key to success in the corps and divisional battle was 'the passage of lines', or passing a fresh unit through an exhausted or battle-shocked unit, to carry on the fight with a new impetus. If this could be done effectively, the commander could get the full fighting value from his reserves: he could maintain control over the action. If the passage of lines was a failure, however, the fresh reserves would be almost useless. They would become mixed up with the troops already fighting, and be infected with their disorganization. The battle would become uncontrollable.

**The Drillbook Theory** for the passage of lines stated that the regiments in the front line should each pull back their flank companies to create gaps between them. The second line would form into battalion columns and march one battalion through each gap. Meanwhile the artillery would redouble its fire to cover this very delicate and risky operation. When the second line had advanced a short way forward it could deploy into line and take up the battle while the original first line either moved back into a continuous line or ployed into columns to march away (*eg* to get more ammunition or to rest, away from the firing line).

Obviously this operation required careful timing, so that the first line was not left with gaps between regiments for longer than absolutely **necessary**, yet the gaps were there when needed. The artillery would also have to be warned when to give covering fire, and the second line would have to be told what to expect when it emerged at the front, bearing the full brunt of the battle. The troops might not need to display the very smartest standards of parade-ground precision, perhaps, but they would at least need to move together on the word of command and have a pretty good idea what was supposed to happen. And in the shock of combat that might not be at all easy.

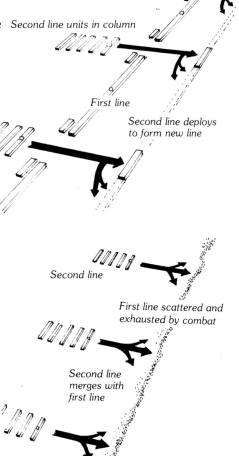

Second line units in column

First line

Second line deploys
to form new line

**In Practice** the passage of lines happened in many different ways, but hardly ever as laid down in the drill book. Quite often the second line would run up to the fighting line in small groups, lie down and open fire while the existing front line troops moved off to the rear. On other occasions the front line would simply break under the strain of combat, or in a panic started by a misunderstood order, and run back through the regiments waiting in reserve behind it. There would then be a grave risk that these too would run with the fugitives, not knowing what terrible dangers there might be to the front.

Quite often the second line reached the first and they all joined in the fight together, making a line of double the previous density, with men of the two units fighting side by side regardless of their normal organization. This had very bad effects on the maneuverability of the troops in combat, since higher control would be lost. The units became little more than milling herds of men, losing their solidity as a formed body. There are several cases of veteran units in the Civil War which flatly refused to be relieved in a passage of lines by raw troops they did not trust, since they feared that this sort of confusion would result. They preferred to fight on alone than to be disorganized by the arrival of reinforcements.

Second line

First line scattered and
exhausted by combat

Second line
merges with
first line

---

## The Indian Rush

One alternative assault tactic, for commanders who did not wish to use massed column attacks, was called the 'Indian Rush'. It consisted of two units or sub-units advancing side by side by alternate bounds. While one fired the other ran forward 50 or 100 yards and then took cover and opened fire while the other advanced, and so on. This was an excellent way of attacking at the same time as fire was brought to bear against the enemy, and it also allowed troops to run forward and then rest before they became too blown. It was rarely used, however, because it needed special training and especially energetic leadership. Co-ordination of the two wings might prove difficult, and the men who went to ground might be just as difficult to push forward again as men who go to ground under fire usually are. What was used a lot more often in the Civil War, and what has confused commentators, was the use of short bounds from one piece of cover to the next by individual skirmishers. This way of advancing and firing was obviously the best way for skirmishers to operate, since each man enjoyed the maximum protection as he came within range. It was often called 'Indian movement', after the wily woodsmen who had originally used it. But without the cohesion and co-ordination of a set piece leapfrogging assault, this skirmishing technique cannot truly be called an 'Indian Rush'.

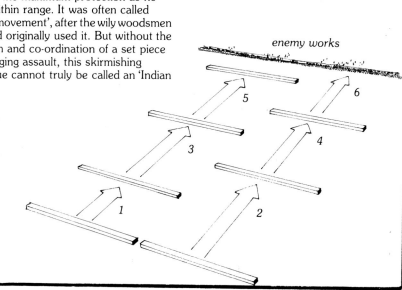

enemy works

**The Petersburg Crater** battle was a classic case of how the passage of lines could go terribly wrong.

The plan was for the Union to fire an enormous mine which they had secretly dug under the Confederate earthworks covering Petersburg. Then a specially-trained assault division of black troops was to storm forward and break through the enemy lines before there was a chance to recover from the shock.

Unfortunately for the carefully-laid plan, however, the black troops were replaced at the last minute by white troops who had received no special training for the assault, who were battle-weary and led by a man who sat out the whole battle in his dug-out in the rear.

The mine exploded late, and when it did the chance of pressing on past the crater was lost. The attacking troops descended into the hole made by the mine, but did not emerge on the far side. They were reinforced first by one and then by another division, but in each case the passage of lines was a failure and the new arrivals simply joined the mass of men in the crater. Finally the black troops were sent in after all, **and their assault drills enabled them to pass** beyond the crater and capture the next enemy line. Alas, control of the battle was then lost, and no reserves were passed through to exploit. Their next attack failed, and the enraged Confederates pushed them back, showing no mercy to the men who had so nearly won a decisive victory.

**Moving a Line** was itself a complex enough operation, even if there was no call for a 'passage' of one line through another. Normally a corps or division commander would hope to form his men in marching column on a road and move like that, wheeling to the flank to occupy a fighting position. If a deployed line had to be moved to a different position, however, they might prefer to form each regiment in a massed column and move across country following oblique routes indicated by staff officers.

**Passing a Defile** always needed extra time and could be complicated if the enemy was close. Once again each regiment would be formed into column, then the central regiments would move through and deploy, followed by those further to the flanks, in turn.

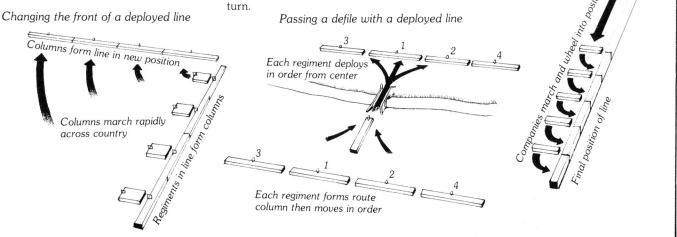

*Changing the front of a deployed line*

Columns form line in new position

Columns march rapidly across country

Regiments in line form columns

*Passing a defile with a deployed line*

3 1 2 4

Each regiment deploys in order from center

3 1 2 4

Each regiment forms route column then moves in order

Companies in route column

Companies wheel and deploy into line

Deployment by wheeling off the march

Companies march and wheel into position

Final position of line

# PART FOUR : THE REGIMENT'S BATTLE

# PREPARING TO FIGHT

Perhaps the tensest time for the soldier came just before he entered combat, in the suspenseful moments when he knew battle was imminent but before its precise shape had become clear. This was the moment for nervous laughter or tight-lipped silence, depending on individual temperament; for **swigging your whiskey or renouncing sin forever. It was a time for checking weapons and discarding useless accoutrements,** even though they might be desperately needed before the day was over.

**The Time to Get Ready** for combat might be mercifully short, if the enemy unexpectedly came swarming over the hill and took you by surprise; or it might be intolerably long if you were alerted for a battle which was put off for hours or even days after it was expected. There was no hard and fast rule for how long would be available.

Old hands said the roadsides leading to a battle would be littered with playing cards discarded by men ashamed to be carrying them, and with particularly heavy items of camp equipment such as kettles and frying pans. There would also be a stream of individuals making to the rear, suddenly overcome by stomach cramps or heat exhaustion ...

Worried men would entrust their wills and other private papers or valuables to their friends. They might pin labels with their names and addresses onto their uniforms, so that in case of death their next of kin could be informed. In some battles arm bands were ordered so that all the men on the same side could be identified in the smoke of combat.

The time before battle was the time for officers to give encouraging speeches, reminding the men of why they were fighting or of the need to aim low. It was the time for extra ammunition to be distributed. 40 rounds was normally carried in each man's

pouch, but an extra 10, 20, even 60 rounds might be loaded onto him when combat was imminent. If extended operations were expected then several days' food would also be handed out, making the soldier more like a pack animal than a light infantryman. On the other hand the order might be given to make a pile of all non-essential luggage, haversacks etc. This would be welcomed if energetic action was definitely imminent, but resented if there was any doubt about it, since these packs were valuable to the **soldier, and no one liked to consign them to** the uncertain chances of war unless there was good cause.

---

**The Regiment** drawn up for battle had its companies in line two deep, numbered off from the right according to position in line, but given a letter according to the senority in rank of the captain. The flank companies might be sent forward as skirmishers; a color party of 9 n.c.o.s' was placed to the left of the 5th company, entrusted with both the safety of the color itself, and with marking the direction of the regiment's alignment by holding it aloft. The company officers stood as 'file closers' immediately to the rear of their commands: the regimental officers were further behind, with any musicians and the medical orderlies, chaplain and other staff.

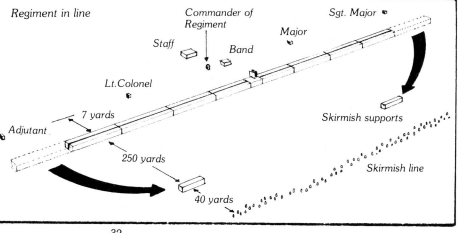

*Regiment in line*

*Staff*  *Lt. Colonel*  *Commander of Regiment*  *Major*  *Band*  *Sgt. Major*

*Adjutant*  7 yards  250 yards  40 yards  *Skirmish supports*  *Skirmish line*

**The Surgeon** of the regiment, if there was one, **organized** spare bandsmen or other details to collect the wounded and bring them for first aid to a point close behind the firing line. Serious cases which could be moved might then be evacuated to division, corps or army aid centers.

**Skulkers** - *ie* those who wished to escape from the battle - were the responsibility first of their buddy group, the four-man team of 'Comrades in Battle' envisaged by the drill manual. If respect for these comrades failed to keep the man in line, the 'File Closers' of company officers standing behind the enlisted men would push him back. If that failed the regimental officers further to the rear might intervene, sometimes even using their weapons. Further in rear there were specially-allocated battle police from the provost department, or roaming cavalry units, with orders to collect stragglers and either punish them summarily or **form** them into *ad hoc* reserve units.

## Infantry Weapons

*percussion musket*

**Muskets** were the old Napoleonic smooth-bore weapons updated since the 1840s by the addition of percussion cap priming instead of flintlock priming. At the start of the war there were four smoothbores available for every rifle, and in the South many soldiers went to war with shotguns or squirrel guns of the most diverse manufacture. Some regiments were armed exclusively with pikes or Bowie knives, due to the shortage of even smoothbore muskets.

By the time of Gettysburg even the well-equipped Union Army of the Potomac still had some 10% of its regiments armed wholly or partially with smoothbores, and at Chickamauga the Confederate Army of Tennessee had over 30%. Nevertheless this weapon could be very devastating at ranges of around 50 yards, particularly if loaded with "buck'n'ball" (combat shotgun) ammunition.

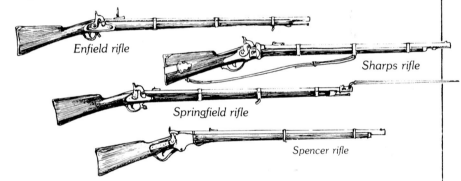

*Enfield rifle*

*Sharps rifle*

*Springfield rifle*

*Spencer rifle*

**Rifles** came in many forms: with round balls (like the muskets); with hollow-base pointed and flanged Minié (or 'Minnie') bullets; with breechloading and even repeating systems. The most widespread infantry arms were the Enfield .577 rifle musket with Minié ball and the highly comparable .58 Springfield M1861 Of the two the Enfield gave a slightly better performance; but the Springfield was available in greater numbers, being 'made in USA'. If we want to find the 'typical' infantry arm of the war it is to these robust, reliable, long range but low velocity and muzzle-loading weapons that we must turn.

Beyond the En- and Spring-fields lay single shot breechloaders such as the Burnside and Sharps. They were equally low velocity (being still black powder weapons), but their rate of fire was greater even if their range and general reliability were less. Beyond them, again, were the death-defying new repeaters (But we must leave them for our discussion of the cavalry, since there were very few infantrymen who could get hold of one in the Civil War).

**The Distribution of Weapons** among infantry regiments in the Civil War is a problem as difficult, in its way, as the classic question "How long is a piece of string?". After an initial issue which might be of various types. Each unit picked up what it could on the battlefield, scrounged what it could from the ordnance services or its neighbours, and lost what it could from the obsolete weapons that it didn't want. Just as in drill and tactics, the regiments went their own way as far as they could within general guidelines that were nevery very precise or rigidly enforced. As an overall rule of thumb allow the following (figures in percentages, based on informed guesswork):-

| Infantry Weapons | Union | | Confederate | |
|---|---|---|---|---|
| | 1862 | 1864 | 1862 | 1864 |
| Smoothbore muskets or worse | 30 | 2 | 60 | 10 |
| 2nd rate rifles | 45 | 13 | 25 | 15 |
| Spring-/En-fields or better | 25 | 85 | 15 | 75 |

**'The Effect of Breakfast'** upon troops entering battle was of dramatic importance. A regiment which had rested and fed before it met the enemy could be guaranteed to fight at least twice as hard as one which had been counter-marching for some time on an empty stomach, particularly in extreme weather conditions.

A major problem with feeding the troops in the Civil War was that it took a considerable time to collect firewood, prepare the necessary items and cook the food (Allow 90-120 minutes for a regiment, 150-180 minutes for a brigade). Old soldiers might have made a point of bringing food which was appetising when eaten cold; but most troops needed the 'sense of occasion' and instant internal warmth of cooking hot food.

# PREPARING THE DEFENSE

Many historians have noted the widespread use of fortifications on Civil War battlefields, even when there was no suggestion of besieging a fortress such as Petersburg or Vicksburg. Civil War officers and soldiers alike seemed to feel that their positions were truly secure only if they had been improved with the spade and the axe. Conversely they were terrified of attacking an enemy line which had been fortified, and by 1864 there was an unwritten agreement between the two sides that 'if you've dug in, you're pretty well fireproof'.

It would be misleading to suppose that fortifications were built as the result of battle experience, however, since some very extensive trench systems were already being constructed in the earliest campaigns of the war - notably the defenses of Washington, Richmond and Fort Donelson, as well as the laborious offensive trench systems dug by McClellan in the Peninsula and Halleck in his approach to Corinth. Soldiers did dig deeper as the war went on; but they had already started digging from the very start.

**Dennis Hart Mahan** was the West Point professor of engineering and the 'science' of war. His classes, apparently, were both terrifying and memorable: they left the generation of officers who fought the Civil War imbued with respect for fortification of every type. Unfortunately there was no higher war school or staff college in America which might have counter-acted this influence with studies of the full range of mobile tactics, and Mahan's engineering doctrine remained the most dominant influence. His son, Alfred Thayer Mahan, was later to win fame as a champion of imperialism based upon sea power .

**The Purpose of Field Fortification is** threefold:-
a) To provide protection against incoming fire, so that unsteady militia troops can be reassured and encouraged to stay in the fight.
b) To place obstacles in the path of an attacker so he will be unable to get to close quarters quickly. If his troops are unsteady militia they will be discouraged and go to ground instead of pressing forward.
c) To provide a cleared field of fire, 50-100 yards wide, in which the defenders can shoot down the attackers. This is especially important if the fieldworks are constructed in woodland where there are no naturally open clearings.

On the other hand the disadvantages of fortification were that they reduced the mobility of friendly troops as much as of the enemy. Even very local counter-attacks became psychologically difficult if they had to cross ditches and ramparts; while if the army felt it needed fieldworks wherever it went, it had to spend a great deal of time and energy building them. Even General Sherman, a great fortification-builder and disciple of Mahan, said that too much sitting in trenches could blunt the attacking spirit of an army.

*50-100 YARDS*

*advanced rifle pits for pickets*

*abatis*

**Wire** was occasionally used to strengthen Civil War entrenchments: *not* the barbed wire of twentieth-century warfare, but plain telegraph wire strung in low-lying entanglements to trip up an attacker. It helped to deter the Confederate attack on Fort Sanders, Knoxville, in 1863 and again at **Bermuda** Hundred in 1864. Nevertheless the effect of wire obstacles on the course of the war can only be called 'negligible'. Wire was in short supply even for the telegraph, and without barbs its full military potential could not be realised. The widespread use of **abatis**, however, provided many defensive systems with a prickly obstacle which had a similar role to more modern barbed wire entanglements.

**Mines** for land warfare came in two different varieties. The classic siege mine consisted of a tunnel dug under the enemy's lines with a heavy charge of powder placed at the end. When the powder was blown the enemy defences were destroyed, as at Petersburg but also in other Civil War sieges.

The more innovative contact mine (called a 'torpedo' in the 1860s) was a relatively small powder charge with a mercury fulminate detonator arranged to explode under the pressure of a man's foot. When camouflaged just below ground the mine made a deadly anti-personnel weapon. A very few of them were used by both sides throughout the Civil War, but they never had much more than scare-value. Both sides denounced them as illegal and immoral at different times - but continued to use them all the same.

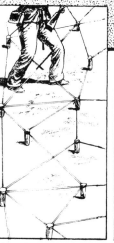

*Fuse*  *Plank*

*Charge*

**Abatis** were trees felled with their tops facing in the direction of the enemy and the tips of the branches sharpened into spikes. One or more lines of closely-packed **abatis** could make a tricky and treacherous obstacle to cross, particularly if they were covered by the defender's fire at close range. Often the attacker went to ground within the abattis and used them for cover - gaining a certain advantage in protection, but failing in his object of pressing on and storming the main trench line. **Abatis** acted as an obstruction to the defender's view of the battlefield (especially if there were still leaves on the felled trees), but in the Civil War most musketry fire was at such short range that this scarcely mattered. We do not hear of range markers being placed at 100 yard intervals in front of Civil War firing lines to help long range accuracy. Instead, we hear of the importance of the final 50-100 yards. If that area was cleared of obstructions the defenders could do all the rifle-shooting they needed.

When there was time to prepare them ( *eg* around Atlanta, 1864), thinner pointed sticks could be used instead of abatis, arranged as **Palisades** or '**Chevaux de Frise**'. These were just as good for delaying an attacker, but gave the defender a clearer view of the battlefield.

Within the trenches themselves there would be room for a man to stand without exposing more than his eyes and his rifle barrel beneath the lumber **Head-Log**. The supporting struts to prevent the headlog rolling back into the trench could also be used to string a pup-tent to make a shelter against the weather.

*headlog*

*palisade*

**Trench Construction** proceeded in stages. The first stage of making a shallow and simple pile of earth or lumber could be done under fire in only a few moments. Next came the more laborious business of scooping out a trench and, if possible, a ditch in front of the parapet. That might take 1 - 2 hours (depending on the type of soil and its moisture), but it could be done even without proper entrenching tools. After this basic entrenching had been completed, there was literally no limit to the improvements which could be made in the ensuing hours or days. Parapets could be raised higher, ditches dug deeper, bombproof shelters built and communication trenches established towards the rear. **Traverses** against enfilading artillery fire were also widely used.

Both sides used black labor to relieve the combat troops from some of the hard work, especially in the case of the more elaborate fortifications. Confederate slave gangs built an especially impressive series of lines during Johnston's phased retreat from Chattanooga to Atlanta.

**Gun Batteries** were more difficult to build than infantry positions, since they required planking on the floor and plenty of protected space for the crews to serve each piece. Sand bags or gabions (wicker baskets filled with earth) could be used when available, to build up the shoulders of the gun embrasure. More normally, however, the crews would have to fight with rather more of their torsos in view of the enemy than they might have wished! They would rely on their fearsome firepower to keep him at bay, rather than upon earthworks.

# THE BREAKDOWN OF TACTICS

The neat and logical theories of the drill sergeant and the tactician almost inevitably broke down at some point during any reasonably intense battle. Human flesh and bone simply could not endure the strain of following the drill precisely for very long, once deadly danger was nearby. The soldiers would follow it only more or less approximately, depending on the level of their training and the imminence of the danger. If they were well - drilled and fresh to battle they would stick to it enthusiastically for a relatively long time. If they were badly drilled, or had seen battle too often, they would quickly throw formal tactics to one side and fight with less effective but more self-serving techniques.

**Men in Battle** tend to have a very restricted field of vision, but intense awareness of the few things they can see *eg* the enemy, the next man in line, the tree stump behind which they are sheltering. They will be aware of constant shouting by officers and n.c.o.s', and the roaring din of musketry. They will not have leisure to keep neat alignments or take a higher view of the way the battle is developing, but will scamper from one piece of cover to another, load, fire and load again as if in a trance. Good soldiers will manage to keep on doing these things despite the terrible danger and the loss of dear friends. Less good soldiers (especially if they have less good n.c.o.s' and officers) will keep their heads down or help their wounded friends to the ambulance or simply drift away to the rear, oblivious to exhortation. If there is a sudden alarm and the start of a rearward movement, the whole line may take it as a valid excuse to run away in panic flight.

**Obstacles** and rough terrain often upset the neat formations of the drill manual, even without the enemy's intervention. A regiment which entered a wood in a line two deep might become scattered into small groups of disoriented individuals within 100 yards. On emerging at the far side it might take many minutes to re-form. Bugle signals could help to keep the troops informed of the regiment's whereabouts, but would be powerless to rally men who took advantage of the foliage to rest or lie low.

The enemy's **abatis** and ditches would add a further opportunity for the reluctant to stay behind while the over-enthusiastic plunged through and offered themselves as isolated, unsupported targets to hostile fire. Officers suffered particularly heavy casualties as a result of this 'sieve' effect which obstacles could exert on a formed body. The obstacles might not be formidable in themselves, but their mere existence so close to the enemy would pose **an extra psychological hurdle which** helped to destroy an attacking unit's cohesion.

**Skulkers** are the men who drop out of battle unwounded, despite the exhortations of their officers. Their departure may be met with sympathy or derision by their comrades, depending on the circumstances, just as it may be followed either by a speedy return to duty or by definitive desertion. Some skulkers simply lay down and hoped the battle would go away - some even went to sleep. Most gathered in the rear **echelon**, around the supply wagons and headquarter staffs. Some became plunderers.

**The Men Who Kept Fighting** did so out of unspoken feelings that it was what they had come to do and what their buddies expected of them. They were anxious not to appear to let their friends down; not to lose face. If the majority seemed to be carrying on with the battle, then the waverers would often do the same. If once a significant group started to the rear, however, it might break the spell and give the waverers the excuse they were looking for. The panic could spread like wildfire, as it did through a whole Confederate brigade at the Bloody Lane, Antietam, or through the unfortunate Union XI Corps at both Chancellorsville and Gettysburg. At Missionary Ridge Bragg's entire army became infected with a similar crowd psychosis. Running away from an unseen and unexplained danger seemed to be the thing to do - so everyone did it together!

**The Smoke and Noise** of battle helped to isolate the individual even further than he had been already by the effects of terrain and fear. Especially when there was no wind, the heavy clouds of smoke from these black-powder weapons could hang over a battlefield for many minutes before dissipating. A regiment of 400 men firing one volley consumed about 3½ lbs powder. A salvo from a four-gun battery consumed 10 lbs. The Union army at Gettysburg used a total of 23 tons of powder, perhaps a ton per hour of combat.

Some of the battles were so noisy they could be heard sixty miles away in still weather, which indicates what it must have been like in the middle of them. On at least one occasion the troops marching through a cotton field picked the cotton to make ear plugs agains the din. On many other occasions we read of officers shouting themselves hoarse in their efforts to be heard, while yelling was an accepted method for helping the soldiers break their tension as much as for impressing the foe.

Experienced officers could learn a great deal about what was happening simply by listening to the level of noise from different types of weapon, and whether the yelling was triumphant or despondent. Before the invention of walkie-talkies this was probably the fastest means available for the course of action to become known.

**Not all soldiers** reacted to battle by standing their ground doggedly or creeping to the rear. Some were spurred forward into acts of reckless bravery, either as individuals or in small groups. This might bring disaster, if the enemy stood his ground and kept firing calmly; or it might be the essential example that was needed to start a major charge, sweeping the enemy away and capturing his works.

**Cover** for men lying prone could usually be found in even apparently open ground. There would be slight contours, friendly fence-rails, welcoming standing crops or shrubbery. Without needing to be told, the soldiers too frightened to advance but too proud to retreat would instinctively seek out these lines of cover. The whole regiment would shake out into a formation determined not by Hardee's drill manual but by the way a farmer had sited his fences or drainage ditches. At Malvern Hill the 22nd Massachusetts used the furrows of a plowed field for cover, with the front rank and second rank each in a furrow of their own. Once they had obtained this minimum of protection they could start to dig in a little deeper with their mess tins, or could start to return the enemy's fire. Command was exercised by officers perched on top of the third furrow, exposed to the enemy. In this way the regiment fired off sixty rounds per man and helped beat off the Confederate attack.

**'The Battle for the Last Hundred Yards'** was often the decisive struggle in the Civil War. Troops could usually be brought to within that distance of an enemy's line, but they could drive off the enemy only if the advance continued to very close quarters. More normally the tension would be too great and the attackers would stop to open fire, regardless of whether or not they had been ordered to do so. Once they had started firing it would be hard to stop them until all their ammunition had been used. On a number of occasions a successful bayonet charge was mounted only after the soldiers had run out of ammunition.

**The Flag** of a regiment was the symbol of its fighting spirit, to be held aloft at all times. In more practical terms it was an aid to unit identification, a direction marker for the regiment's movement or the rallying point if the regiment became scattered. It was a great disgrace if the flag was captured by the enemy; but a correspondingly great triumph if his fell into the regiment's hands.

The strength of an enemy's force could be estimated by the number of regimental colors he was flying, and of course each one served as a convenient aiming mark. The color bearer's position was the most dangerous in the regiment, and in many hard-fought battles the flag changed hands several times as successive bearers were hit.

# THE FIREFIGHT

Shooting at the enemy was the natural response of the infantry soldier who came under the enemy's fire. It allowed the individual to do something which satisfied the demands of his fear and of his adrenalin. Firing was a positive act, even if it couldn't actually hit anyone, in a way that marching forward without giving fire was not. Attacking troops who came near the enemy were therefore more likely to stop and shoot than they were to press on in a bayonet charge. This was doubly true in view of the widespread belief in fortifications which was held by most of the soldiers. Even though firing was the principal means of combat, the astonishing fact is that few Civil War regiments did very much target practice, and still fewer did it systematically. The battles therefore consisted of prolonged blazing away between two groups of men who could not shoot straight!

**In close order** formations there was a problem with musketry, since the men were so tightly packed in the ranks that they obstructed each other and made loading difficult. The men in the second rank also had to take special care not to singe or even shoot the men in the front rank. Many accidents are recorded, and a high proportion must have been due to this cause. Although psychological pressures may have led the men to bunch closely together for reassurance, the practical pressures were to thin out the firing line and give everyone freedom to load and shoot.

**Drill Training** in loading procedures was given to every soldier, but usually without the chance to fire live ammunition before the battle itself. Many men were found to be entirely unfamiliar with firearms, and there seems to be little evidence that the average American was 'born and bred' with a rifle by his side. In the excitement of combat a high proportion of soldiers made mistakes in their loading sequence, thereby making it impossible to use that rifle for the rest of the battle.

**A kneeling or prone** posture was usually adopted in a firefight unless there was cover (eg a trench) sufficiently high to protect a standing man. The drill manuals did actually recommend methods for loading when prone or kneeling, but it must still have been a complex and awkward process. The total length of a rifle musket plus ramrod extended for ramming amounted to no less than 8 feet! In these circumstances it is surprising if the normal rate of fire of the infantryman in battle was low.

**Fire Control** was practically non-existent in the infantry line. Assuming the officer could be heard and obeyed at all, his instructions would normally be little more than to open and cease fire, and to 'aim at their belt buckles' or 'aim at their knees' (because the tendency was to shoot too high). Although rifle muskets had accurate leaf sights calibrated up to 1,000 yards, there seems little evidence that these were adjusted in battle except by a small minority of crack shots. Usually the idea was to wait until the range was so close that such refinements were superfluous - at true 'point blank' range, in fact.

The first shot was often fired as a volley by companies or by the whole regiment, but after that it was only the very best troops who could continue firing volleys on the word of command. Almost always the fire became a 'fire at will' after the first shot - and the drill manual actually recommended that this should be ordered.

**The Loading Sequence** was as follows:- 'Load' (holding the rifle vertically in front of the body), 'Handle Cartridge' (taking it from pouch), 'Tear Cartridge' (between teeth), 'Charge Cartridge' (pouring powder into muzzle, followed by bullet and paper), 'Draw Rammer', 'Ram Cartridge', 'Return Rammer', 'Prime' (place percussion cap on nipple), 'Shoulder Arms', 'Ready' (pointing at enemy and cocking), 'Aim', 'Fire'.

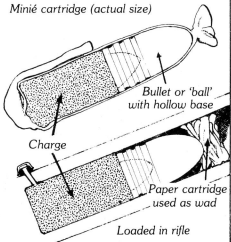

*Minié cartridge (actual size)*

*Bullet or 'ball' with hollow base*

*Charge*

*Paper cartridge used as wad*

*Loaded in rifle*

**Rebel Marksmen** had a considerable reputation for straight shooting, on the assumption that peacetime Southern society accustomed its members to the use of firearms more than did the urban North. There are certainly plenty of anecdotes of spectacular feats by individuals (**eg** the officer who shot 20 Yankees in one skirmish; the man who pipped a Yankee at 1,000 yards, and so on). Both sides had snipers and sharpshooter units, however, so this is scarcely conclusive. Rather more **telling is the fact that the Confederates had** much less ammunition to spare than the North, so they had to be more careful about the way they used it. They would often take

**The rate of fire** varied enormously, depending on circumstances. Although the drill book envisaged over three rounds per minute it is improbable that this was ever approached in a real battle for a period longer than a minute. It would normally take 40-120 minutes for each man to fire off his forty rounds, and on many occasions this could be strung out much longer. Conversely if the enemy did not retreat after the initial few shots (fired quickly from clean rifles) it would be unlikely that the shots which followed would make much impression. The battle would gradually die away unless either side was reinforced or launched an attack.

**The military effectiveness** of a unit engaged in a firefight came from the impression of danger that it conveyed to the enemy. If the unit **made** plenty of smoke, flame and noise it would seem to be very dangerous and the enemy would not wish to come closer. With Minié bullets particularly there would be an impressive whistling noise even if the shot itself was very wide of the mark. With breechloading rifles and carbines the rate of fire could be significantly faster than with muzzle loaders, and hence the effect proportionally greater. In general the better-nourished the fire, the more frightening it would be to the enemy.

longer aiming each shot, and get more hits per round fired as a result. This is not to say that they scored more hits per hour in a firefight, merely that they did so with less ammunition than their Union opponents. Against this we must also note that the

effectiveness of fire in **demoralizing** the enemy often had as much to do with the number of shots fired as it did with accuracy, so in practical terms the Union may not have suffered great disadvantages by its high ammunition consumption.

**At Marye's Heights** in the battle of Fredericksburg, 1862, the Union attack went to ground in a slight fold in the ground some 100-250 yards short of the Confederates. The Northern soldiers established a firing line and used up their ammunition. More regiments were sent to their support and joined in, redoubling the fire and cramming the line with men. Few of them remembered, however, that they had been sent to attack Marye's Heights, not simply to shoot at them. The firefight sucked them up and made them forget their attack. Some of them stayed there, firing occasionally, for over two days!

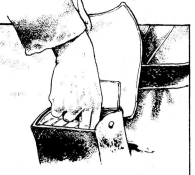

### Anatomy of a Firefight
Some vital statistics of the 'typical' Civil War firefight, assuming one regiment of 400 men on each side and reasonably open terrain. The Confederate attackers have 30 rounds per man, the Union defenders 50.

|  | Case One - Spring 1862 | Case Two - Fall 1864 |
|---|---|---|
| Confederate armament | 350 Smoothbore muskets<br>30 Shotguns<br>20 Bowie knives | 395 Enfield rifle muskets<br>5 Breechloaders |
| Union armament | 400   .69 M1842 Rifled muskets | 400 Springfield rifles |
| Range at which US opens fire | 150 yards | 250 yards |
| Range at which CS reply | 100 yards | 150 yards |
| Range at which CS halt | 40 yards | 50 yards |
| Hits on CS in firefight | 110 | 110 |
| Hits on US in firefight | 90 | 90 |
| Duration of firefight (**eg** until all rounds fired) | 60 minutes | 120 minutes |
| Hence US hit per minute | 1.8 Confederates | 0.9 Confederates |
| CS hit per minute | 1.5 Federals | 0.7 Federals |
| Average US hits per round fired | 0.0055 hits (= 181 rounds per hit) | 0.0055 hits (= 181 rounds per hit) |
| Average CS hits per round fired | 0.0079 hits (= 127 rounds per hit) | 0.0075 hits (= 133 rounds per hit) |

# THE BAYONET CHARGE

The aim of a bayonet charge was to destroy the cohesion of an enemy unit and chase it away. Any casualties which might be inflicted on it in the process were seen as incidental to the main purpose of breaking the solidity of its line. Hence the bayonet was not intended as a weapon for killing, like the rifle, but as a weapon for winning decisive results.

Many (but not all) Civil War officers understood this, and many successful bayonet attacks were carried out. Nevertheless it was often difficult to persuade soldiers to leave the safety of cover (especially fortifications) to risk their lives in a charge. They usually felt happier keeping their heads down and shooting at the enemy rather than in finishing the battle quickly by a decisive act.

**Bayonets were fixed,** usually, only when the moment came for charging. To fix them earlier would interfere with loading and shooting. Hence the order to 'Fix Bayonets' had a special significance as the mark of a serious determination to overrun the enemy. It was equivalent to that other thrilling, fateful order - 'Packs down - charge!'. The soldier would be very reluctant to abandon his personal baggage on the battlefield, especially if there were inadequate arrangements for guarding it. Hence the order to jettison packs in order to speed an attack was full of significance.

**The alleged uselessness of the bayonet** in the eyes of many historians rests upon statistics which show that it caused only a negligible number of wounds in combat. We often read of soldiers throwing their bayonets away, and even charging the enemy with only the bare muzzles of their rifles. In any case, it is argued, the firefight was far and away the most important tactical event on the Civil War battlefield - not the bayonet charge.

It is quite true that most troops preferred to shoot rather than to charge, but that is to miss the fact that the best troops *would* charge when ordered. Hood's Texans at Gaines's Mill successfully cleared a *very* strong defensive position without stopping to fire: two years later he in turn was defeated at Nashville by a series of Union attacks which gave fire as they advanced, but did not go to ground.

The concept of **Shock Tactics** could be used in defense as well as in the attack. If a defender lay low until an attacker was almost upon him, then sprang up, gave a volley and a yell followed by a bayonet charge, there was an excellent chance of success. The idea was to numb the enemy psychologically by a rapid series of unexpected events - not by a predictable and protracted firefight which might cost many casualties but achieve nothing.

Admittedly the bayonet itself was only one element in shock tactics, paralysing the enemy no more than the surprise volley or the menacing yell. The bayonet was useless if the troops carrying it were poorly led, by officers who did not understand maneuver or surprise. Yet in combination with these other elements of success the bayonet was a powerful symbol of decisive action and major results. It was only a pity that this was not more widely understood in the 1860s.

**Bayonets had many uses** apart from their intended use as weapons. They made custom-built candle sticks and excellent skewers for cookery. Troops without entrenching tools could use them to loosen the earth when digging in. If bent round, they provided hooks for hanging utensils over a fire.

At the start of the war many soldiers took Bowie knives along as a general purpose auxiliary implement, but this practice declined as other items became more important - especially axes, machetes, picks and spades for making fortifications.

**The medical records** from the Army of the Potomac in the spring campaign of 1864 (from the Wilderness to Petersburg) show that out of about 50,000 men hit by enemy action about 25 (0.05%) were victims to sword blows and about 50 (0.1%) to bayonet thrusts. Only 11% of these wounds were fatal, as opposed to around 20% to all causes.

We must approach these statistics with caution, since the 1864 campaign can scarcely be seen as typical of the war as a whole. The troops had passed their prime as aggressive, enterprising attackers, and we may speculate that comparable statistics for earlier years of the war would have given a higher proportion of bayonet wounds. Nevertheless the general picture is certainly true that musketry (including musketry delivered in successful bayonet charges) accounted for vastly more casualties than the *arme blanche*.

**Yells, shouts and cheers** were used by most units as a means of releasing tension and scaring the enemy. When a hostile force had been beaten there would be triumphant yelling; when a friendly force had been defeated the yells would be defiant. Most of all, perhaps, the yell would be used in the attack to help charging troops to keep up their momentum. In close country such as the Wilderness we hear of some attacks which succeeded because the enemy imagined a far bigger force, estimated from the yells, than was actually threatening them. Only a few officers (*eg* Sherman) disapproved of yelling in the attack, preferring a grim and silently menacing approach rather than the wild indiscipline of a yelling charge. Others were prepared to sacrifice even surprise and concealment in order to allow their men a

good yell (*eg* Hancock's attack at Spotsylvania, covered by morning mist, revealed its presence by yelling on command at 600 yards from the enemy).

Most famous was the whooping, warbling 'Rebel Yell' which could be sustained for minutes on end - 'Whoa-Whoa-Whoa-

Whoa!' passing back and forth along the Confederate line and striking dread into Union hearts. But there were many different variants, both North and South (*eg* 'Three Times Three For Tennessee!' or 'Go In Baltimore!': almost every state had its characteristic yell).

**Bayonet Drill** was far more common in the Civil War than target practice with live ammunition. McClellan had translated a French bayonet fencing manual in 1852, and there were several alternative systems available. These drills were formalised, demanding correct posture and sprightly footwork for both thrusting and parrying - all based on the assumption that the enemy would be sportingly fencing with his bayonet on the other side. In reality troops who came to close quarters were more likely to fire their rifles or use the butts as clubs, rather than to follow the elegant choreography of the fencing-masters.

**Close combat** was relatively rare in the Civil War, since attacks which didn't go to ground would usually persuade a defender to run away before contact was made. If he did not run, one of two things might happen. Either the attacker would go to ground after all, maybe as close as five yards away. Firefights lasting several hours were sometimes conducted between two forces standing on either side of the same earth parapet. Alternatively if the attacker kept advancing there would be genuine hand to hand combat, using any weapons available. At Second Manassas the Confederates took to throwing rocks at their attackers, while in some of the trench fighting around Petersburg spades were used. Such fighting could never continue for long, however, and one side or the other would soon break and run.

# CAVALRY

For the first three years of the war the cavalry was used for scouting and raiding far more than it was for battle. Very few charges were made against infantry, and always on such a small scale that they were easily defeated. By 1864, however, a more effective battlefield use was starting to be found for cavalry, especially on the Union side. By combining mounted action with fighting on foot, the horse soldiers began to make an impact on the operations of the infantry. By the time of the final Appomattox campaign this impact had turned into a decisive, war-winning tactical method.

**American cavalry tactics,** as they had emerged by 1864, were quite different from classic European tactics of massed charges by whole brigades or divisions. In the Civil War a cavalry regiment might deploy two thirds of its strength as dismounted skirmishers - *ie* 'Mounted Infantry' - to probe the enemy and engage him in a firefight. The Union cavalry had an especial advantage in this, since their modern repeating carbines gave them a high rate of fire which boosted the shock value of a dismounted attack. Often their dismounted firing line could chase off the enemy simply by walking forward firing: what today is called 'Marching Fire'. On the Confederate side there was much less of the latest technology available, but with Enfield rifles and carbines a dismounted line could still be formidable.

If the firing line failed to make progress it could at least discover the enemy's weak points, and could clear avenues of approach for a mounted charge. Fences could be removed to allow the remaining one third of

the regiment to rush upon the enemy with sabers or revolvers. This often worked well and even fortifications could sometimes be cleared by a saber charge which had been properly prepared!

Finally, if neither dismounted nor mounted action succeeded in breaking the enemy, the whole regiment could retire a **short way, mount up and maneuver rapidly** around the enemy's flank or rear to cut him off. The cavalry had far more options open to it than the infantry.

**General Philip H Sheridan** was the man most centrally responsible for the reform of the Union cavalry in 1864, when he came to the Army of the Potomac from the Western theater. Young, energetic and resourceful, he believed that concentrated cavalry/mounted infantry could overcome any opposition. First against Early in the Shenandoah Valley, and then in the Appomattox campaign the following year, he proved this was no idle boast. He used his cavalry as the spearhead of what we would today call a *blitzkrieg* or lightning war. The cavalry moved for the enemy's flank and hoped to scatter the hastily-assembled forces which could be thrown in its path. Meanwhile supporting infantry would make forced marches to occupy the ground won, or provide heavy back-up if the cavalry had

encountered serious opposition. Even if the initial combats were not particularly successful (as they were not in the Appomattox campaign at Dinwiddie Courthouse), the cavalry's mobility could be used to disengage and strike from a fresh direction soon afterwards. The enemy would be faced with a bewildering succession of unexpected blows, and his staffwork would be stretched to the limit in meeting them. His army would have to march and counter march in different directions: its cohesion would be eroded. Isolated detachments could be surprised and overwhelmed (*eg* at Sayler's Creek in 1865), and then finally the attacking cavalry would cut off the line of retreat of the main body, allowing the following infantry to complete an encirclement (*eg at* Appomattox Courthouse itself).

**Organization:** The cavalry started the war in individual regiments, but these were later brought together into brigades, divisions and even complete cavalry corps. In Wilson's 1865 Selma campaign his force of 15,000 men did not include a single infantryman.

The regiment was composed of 5 squadrons each of 2 companies and an average of around 80 men. They formed in line two deep, with commissioned officers ahead and most n.c.o's in the front line. The Union regiments soon switched to 12 companies per regiment organized in three battalions of two squadrons each. The Confederates stayed with the original configuration until numbers declined in the last two years of war. When this happened the regiment re-

duced the number of its squadrons while keeping each one as nearly up to strength as possible. The tactical unit for the Union was at first the squadron, but as regiments gradually shrank, the battalion took over.

Cavalry regiments usually operated in a column of squadrons for ease of maneuver in broken terrain; sometimes it was a column of companies, at other times a line of squadrons in column. Rarely was a fully deployed line of a whole regiment seen in combat.

In 1864 the Union cavalry in the West adopted the 1861 Cooke drill manual, which used a single rank within each squadron, instead of the double rank advocated by the existing (1841) regulations.

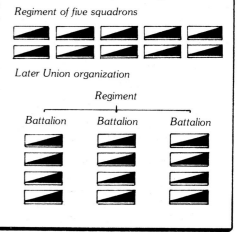

*Confederate and early Union organization*

*Regiment of five squadrons*

*Later Union organization*

Regiment

*Battalion*    *Battalion*    *Battalion*

**Cavalry Weapons** were many and varied, ranging from straight thrusting swords to curved slashing swords, and from 'militarised' farm shotguns to antique single shot smoothbore pistols and carbines. It soon became obvious, however, that the favourite hardware for mounted combat was to be the latest Colt revolver. A hard-fighting horseman might have as many as five of these distributed around his accoutrements, if he could get hold of them. For dismounted combat an infantry rifle was carried or - better still - a breechloading carbine. The Sharps and Burnside both gave good performance, and the ageing Hall was still not to be despised. But there is no doubt that it was the Henry and Spencer repeaters which were the most prized and coveted (firing 15 and 7 rounds at a loading, respectively). In terms of ballistics and reliability these were not particularly impressive guns: but their unprecedented rate of fire in a 'mad minute' made up for everything.

**The Confederate Cavalry** enjoyed a marked superiority over its Union opponents for perhaps the first three years of the war, before the tide turned. Under dashing leaders such as Ashby and Stuart they established a superiority in *morale*, horsemanship and simple boldness. Their weakness lay in their indiscipline and highly 'personal' attitude to the war. Because they had to provide their own horse and weaponry they felt they were entitled to go home when they pleased. General J E B Stuart also missed his chance of creating a genuine battlefield role for his troopers, preferring to chase after booty in long range raiding, instead.

**Cavalry as 'Vampyres'**: Stuart's example of daring raids behind enemy lines set a fashion for both sides for the remainder of the war. It became an established principle that cavalry was better employed in this type of activity than in either the massed battlefield combat known to the Europeans, or the semi-strategic mounted-infantry 'spearhead' role favoured by Sheridan. Raiding became a way of life and a way of personal enrichment for many horse soldiers.

What happened when a large force of cavalry went a-raiding? Normally there would be a difficult approach march as the raiders maneuvered to insert themselves in the enemy's rear echelon without having to fight their way in. Much depended upon speed and surprise, leaving all too little time for horse care or the finer points of *etiquette* towards the local population. Next came a series of attacks against supply dumps, railroads and 'government property' (including the property of 'suspected possible supporters of the government'). Each of these targets might be more or less well defended, giving the raid its particular spice; although normally the opposition could be overcome quickly and the raiders could enjoy the full benefits traditionally accorded to any small group of armed men who successfully dominate a rich and extensive civilian zone. Finally would come the ride home with bulging saddlebags, exhausted horses but pride in a job well done - a job of plunder and destruction.

**The strategic value of raiding** was often quite minor, despite the adulation showered upon such enterprises as Wilson's Selma campaign or (with a force composed mostly of infantry) Sherman's march to the sea. J E B Stuart himself was not free from the accusation that he won more glory than solid benefit for the Confederacy, while Stoneman's raid during the Chancellorsville battle achieved little more than the removal of its cavalry from the Union army at the moment it was needed most.

Nevertheless there were enough examples of 'strategically useful' raiding to keep the game alive in the minds of higher commanders. In particular the Confederate cavalry in the Western theater during the first three years of war played havoc with the Union railroads, and had a serious impact upon logistics. This in turn meant that many of the planned Union offensives had to be delayed or even abandoned. There was a disproportionate relationship between the small number of the raiders, and the great importance of their mission, which exerted a magical influence upon the generals of both sides. Grant was possibly the worst affected, since his own wife had been kidnapped in one of these raids; but the Confederates were no less mesmerised. The exploits of Wheeler, Morgan, Quantrill and Forrest passed into legend, even though their activities were sometimes difficult to distinguish from highway robbery. After the war Jesse James based his career of crime upon his experiences in the Quantrill gang, while Forrest went on to found the Ku Klux Klan.

# NIGHT AND FOG

In twentieth century warfare we have learned to exploit night and fog in combat, and when they are not available we have smoke screens on call to make good the deficiency. In the Civil War, by contrast, all this was regarded as rather heretical. Troops who tried to maneuver at night usually got lost, mistook friends for enemies, and became disastrously short of sleep. There were simply too many possible sources of confusion in low visibility to make warfare an attractive proposition. By an unwritten mutual agreement commanders on both sides preferred to fight when the sun was shining and everyone had at least a fighting chance of following what was going on.

The first major exception to this rule was the night march, when commanders tried to outmaneuver their opponents, or steal a march upon them, under cover of darkness. This could sometimes be successful, but is was certainly exhausting for the soldiers. The second case arose in a battle when a decisive result had not been reached when dusk fell. In those circumstances firing might continue long into the night.

**Dusk** usually came too soon for the successful commander who wanted to press on and reap the fruits of victory - but by the same token it often came as a welcome relief to a hard-pressed army on the verge of collapse. Sometimes the troops took the onset of darkness as a clear sign that it was time to cease fire, but more often at the end of a hard-fought day there would be a final flourish of hostilities. Intermittent, formless skirmishing might continue for a while before both sides settled down to rest - or perhaps to sneak silently away.

Dusk was a time of errors and confusion. It was then that Stonewall Jackson was accidentally shot by his own troops in the Chancellorsville woods, and then that Ewell's attacks on the second day of Gettysburg went awry and degenerated into a nightmare of blind firing in the dark. Only occasionally, as at the Bloody Angle at Spotsylvania, did dusk apparently make no difference. On that occasion the 'smoke-laden rain' had made visibility difficult enough in daylight. When dusk fell the battle continued unabated until 3 am.

**Night Fighting** was a specialist art which lacked manuals or training courses in the 1860s. When it was attempted it usually led to confusion, particularly if more than one regiment was involved. Nevertheless there were some examples of small but highly successful night attacks, notably some of the Confederate trench raids around Kenesaw and Atlanta. On at least two occasions the best part of a Union regiment was captured in its sleep by a well organized team which first crept up to capture the pickets, then sent shock troops through to the main line. This was exemplary bloodless warfare which modern Special Forces might envy!

**Mistaken Identity** was a major hazard throughout the Civil War. As early as First Manassas some positions were captured because the defenders mistook enemy soldiers for friends, and as late as the Appomattox campaign there were still some firefights between friendly units who each imagined the others were enemy. 'Uniforms' were too varied and drab for any certainty of recognition, and although flags offered more hope not even they could be decoded in low visibility or if they were furled. Outposts used a system of passwords to identify newcomers, but it was far from foolproof. 'Blue on Blue' (or 'Gray on Gray') combat was never completely eradicated.

**Dawn** is the time at which an attacker can approach under cover of darkness, launch a surpise assault in the deceptive half light, then beat off counter-attacks in full daylight. Throughout military history it has always been a dangerous moment for a defender.

In the Civil War there were a number of dawn surpises, although the overstretched Confederates before Atlanta and Petersburg sometimes criticized their Union opponents for missing golden opportunities. At Cedar Creek, October 1864, General Early's men made no such mistake, and completely surprised two Union camps from flank and rear.

As in any night-time operation, a dawn surprise needs careful planning. The approach routes must be reconnoitered and each man briefed on his role. Sometimes this will require lying out close to the enemy for some time without making a noise. There may be signal guns to mark the start of the attack, and arm bands or other identification signs to help recognition. In really well-organized attacks some troops will be detailed to move outwards from the breakthrough point while others move forward to exploit. This technique could work well provided there was plenty of time for training and preparation.

**'Jack O' Lanterns' or 'Will O' The Wisps'** sometimes deceived sentries posted in swampy terrain, with their flickering, elusive lights. A man's imagination could certainly play tricks when he was watching for the enemy through the darkest part of a night. Noises could be magnified out of all proportion; the sentry would start to full wakefulness, and might shoot. This in turn could arouse the whole regiment and there might be a 'firefight' against a purely imaginary foe. Armies close to the enemy suffered many **disturbed** nights in this way.

**Fog or morning mist** was a feature of some Civil War battles, supplementing the smoke of gunpowder and helping to muffle sound. At Fredericksburg the mist interfered with Burnside's wig wag communications but later helped him to conceal the retreat of his army. His critics complain that he ought also to have exploited it to conceal his frontal assault on the enemy lines, which was sent forward in broad daylight and suffered accordingly.

At Lookout Mountain, 'the battle above the clouds', the Union troops did successfully exploit the heavy mist to conceal some of their movements, but suffered from it later when it prevented Grant's HQ from seeing how the attack was progressing.

Only when a gust of wind momentarily blew aside the clouds could success be assessed. It was better than hoped, and a great cheer rose from the 30,000 men waiting below! In mid afternoon the battle closed down 'because the mist was too thick' according to Northerners, or 'because the Yankees were whipped' according to Confederates.

**The Camp Fire** had a special importance for the Civil War soldier. It was his means of cooking food, and in winter the source of his warmth. It was a social focus and a reassuring influence in a harsh and uncomfortable world. The army as a whole could draw further comfort from the huge number of its **fires,** which if seen from a distance could resemble the street lights of a major city. This in turn allowed the enemy to estimate the numbers and positions of the army he faced, although he had to beware of deception. A small force might make itself look bigger by building additional fires, or a retreating force might cover its movement by building fires to give the impression it was settling down for the night. Troops holding positions too close to the enemy, however,

would often be given the infuriating order not to light fires at all, in case they illuminated targets for marksmen or otherwise gave too much away.

Fire can sometimes run out of control, and in some Civil War battles artillery muzzle flashes set the woods alight and started an uncontrollable inferno. At Chancellorsville and again in the Wilderness battles the immobilised wounded were engulfed horrifically in fires of this sort. At Atlanta the fires which were deliberately started to burn down 'some' of the buildings ran out of control and destroyed 'most' of them. It was, after all, a policy of 'scorched earth' that Sherman set out to bring to the South.

# THE AFTERMATH OF BATTLE

A battle was, to say the least, an awesome thing to be mixed up in. Yet when the firing stopped and the participants came to count the cost, it was usually **realized** that the sacrifice had been terrible indeed.

Some men did well out of battle, if plunder was plentiful or promotion to be had as a result of casualties among higher officers. General Grant won the highest promotion of all as a result of his years of battling - he was twice elected to the presidency of the United States.

For many it was reward enough simply to survive a battle unscathed. The ordeal was frightening beyond any civilian experience, and its results were shocking enough to turn even the strongest stomach. *"I dont Waunt to see it no more I am satsfied with Ware"* wrote one Alabama soldier after witnessing the battle of Murfreesboro.

For all too many, though, battle led to disaster or death. Those who were killed outright were often luckier than the lingering wounded or the prisoners destined to long months in an insanitary and under-fed concentration camp. Some of the wounded recovered quickly; but all too many of them were scarred forever.

**Clearing Up** after a battle could be a long process, and it provided a powerful reason not to move away from the scene for some time after the firing had ceased. The following tasks had to be performed:-
1) Rally scattered regiments and re-group them as effective fighting units. Top up their supplies of ammunition, food and water. Re-allocate command appointments where officers have been lost. Count your new fighting strength.
2) Care for as many of the wounded as possible, especially those of your own side who look as though they may live, and of course any commissioned officer.
3) Salvage anything useful from the field, especially money, shoes and modern weapons. This process included turning out the pockets of the dead, the wounded and the prisoners. Most items had a saleable value, whether it was a greatcoat, a gold watch or a set of harness.
4) Write home to reassure your family that you have survived, or to explain to your buddy's family the circumstances of his death. The bodies of the wealthy would be embalmed and returned to their families; those of the rest would be buried in shallow graves or not at all. Friends might leave improvised markers on graves, but durable momuments would be erected only in later decades.
5) Collect the prisoners and send them to the rear. Feed them if there are supplies to spare. Shoot them if they try to escape. Eventually you will hope to exchange them for prisoners captured by the enemy, although from 1864 onwards the Union stopped this practice, arguing that the South could not replace its combat losses from its population, whereas the North could. This policy meant there was a build-up of numbers in the prison camps, and hence an escalating death toll among them.
6) Deal with disciplinary cases arising from the battle - officers who defied orders, commissaries who were too scared to bring their ammunition into the firing line, soldiers who tried to desert. A blind eye would often be turned amid the relief of stress after combat; but it was usually felt that an example would have to be made of the more blatant cases.

**Casualties** in Civil War battles were not especially high by Napoleonic or First World War standards, but they were quite high enough. An army which accepted the risk of combat could expect to lose 10%, 20% or even 30% of its fighting strength, regardless of whether it won or lost. A representative selection of losses is shown in this table:-

| Battle and date | Attacker | Winner | Confederate Loss | Union Loss |
|---|---|---|---|---|
| | | | (+ rough totals of killed, wounded, missing loss as percentage of total force present) | |
| First Manassas, July '61 | US | CS | 2,000 (11%) | 2,900 (16%) |
| Shiloh, April '62 | CS | US | 10,700 (25%) | 13,000 (22%) |
| Seven Pines, May '62 | CS | US | 5,800 (14%) | 4,500 (13%) |
| Gaines's Mill, June '62 | CS | CS | 9,000 (17%) | 4,000 (14%) |
| Malvern Hill, July '62 | CS | US | 9,000 (12%) | 5,000 (6%) · |
| Second Manassas, September '62 | US | CS | 10,000 (18%) | 14,000 (22%) |
| Antietam, September '62 | US | CS | 10,000 (25%) | 12,000 (25%) |
| Perryville, October '62 | CS | US | 3,300 (19%) | 4,000 (12%) |
| Murfreesboro, December '62 | CS | US | 10,000 (27%) | 13,000 (29%) |
| Fredericksburg, December '62 | US | CS | 5,300 (7%) | 12,000 (12%) |
| Chancellorsville, May '63 | CS | CS | 13,000 (18%) | 17,000 (16%) |
| Champion's Hill, May '63 | US | US | 2,200 (11%) | 2,500 (12%) |
| Gettysburg, July '63 | CS | US | 21,000 (29%) | 23,000 (27%) |
| Chickamauga, September '63 | CS | CS | 18,000 (26%) | 16,000 (26%) |
| Chattanooga, November '63 | US | US | 6,700 (18%) | 5,800 (10%) |
| Wilderness, May '64 | US | CS | 5,000 (8%) | 17,000 (18%) |
| Spotsylvania, May '64 | US | CS | 8,000 (13%) | 18,500 (20%) |
| Atlanta, July '64 | CS | US | 10,000 (20%) | 4,000 (8%) |
| Petersburg Crater, July '64 | US | CS | 1,000 (10%) | 3,800 (26%) |
| Nashville, December '64 | US | US | 8,000 (24%) | 3,000 (6%) |
| Bentonville, March '65 | US | US | 2,600 (20%) | 1,600 (8%) |

**The Execution of Deserters** was a doleful proceeding which most Civil War soldiers witnessed at least once in their military careers, especially on the Confederate side (where the scanty reserves of manpower made desertion a more serious offense). Normally a whole division would be formed up in horseshoe formation, and the condemned man (or men) placed in front of the firing squad on the open side. It was a solemn and memorable moment, which never failed to move the witnesses - who had perhaps remained unmoved at the sight of many more horrifying casualties in battle.

As a percentage of total deserters, however, the number executed was tiny - well under 1%. Deserters were more likely to be struck down by the battle police in the heat of combat itself, and we can say that the further away from the firing line they went, the safer they became. Civil War armies were relatively tolerant and humane institutions, by European standards, when it came to treatment of their own criminals or of civilians. But then, European standards in these matters were themselves appallingly low.

**Prisoners** were most at risk at the moment when they tried to surrender. There was no certainty that an enraged enemy in the flush of fierce action would accept the surrender, especially if the surrendering man belonged to certain especially-hated categories. To Confederate soldiers any black found fighting for the North, and especially his white officers, fell into this group. For both sides the practitioner of 'underhand' means of warfare was also given a hard time - *eg* the man who planted a ground mine or who fired an explosive bullet. In certain campaigns particular units, or the troops of a particular commander, gained evil reputations which had to be avenged in blood.

Once surrender had been accepted, however, the front line soldiers behaved reasonably chivalrously to their captives. It was only as he was shunted to the rear that the prisoner's problems reappeared.

As for **The Wounded**, their first problem was to find their way to an aid post. If they could not manage to do this in a relatively short time they risked death by exposure to climatic extremes, loss of blood, dehydration or murder by plunderers. If they did succeed in reaching aid they had an 86% chance of survival - although the frequent use of amputation might well deprive them of a limb. 71% of wounds were to limbs, while 11% of the remainder were to face, head or neck (The total number of hits on the latter areas was almost double that, however, since far more of them were fatal than were wounds elsewhere).

**Hospitals** were frightening places, often overcrowded, insanitary and wracked with infectious diseases. They were ill-equipped to sort out the complex fractures typically caused by Minié bullets, and still less well equipped to combat gangrene. If they could cope with their patients (more or less) in normal times, that probably meant they would be quite incapable of dealing with the enormous influx of critical cases which resulted from a battle - assuming that these had survived the horrific, jolting journey from the battlefield at all.

The Civil War was fought in the age before truly scientific medicine, let alone before truly scientific *combat* medicine (which may be dated to the age of the helicopter). Tens of thousands of men died who could and should have been saved : tens of thousands died of neglect who might have pulled through with the help of a little tender loving care.

# FURTHER READING

## GENERAL HISTORIES

Adams, M **Our Masters the Rebels** (Harvard University 1978 - for the evolution of *morale* in the East; **Battles and Leaders** (ed. Johnson & Buel, Century Co, New York, 4 Vols 1884 and many reprints); Catton, B - his classic series from **Mr Lincoln's Army** (New York 1951) to **Grant Takes Command** (New York 1968); Esposito, V J **The West Point Atlas of the Civil War** (New York); Hattaway, H and Jones, A **How The North Won** (University of Illinois 1983); Livermore, T L **Numbers and Losses in the Civil War** (New edn., Indiana University 1957 - for casualty statistics); Mitchell, J B **Decisive Battles of the Civil War** (Fawcett edn, New York 1962); **Official Records of the War of the Rebellion** (US War Department, Washington, 128 Vols, 1880-1901 - the definitive collection of Civil War documents, to be used only if one has a lifetime free for study!)

## TACTICS

**Battles Lost and Won** (ed. Hubbell, J T, Westport Conn. 1975 - a splendid collection of specialist articles); Griffith, P **Rally Once Again** (Chichester, England 1986) Luvaas, J **The Military Legacy of the Civil War** (Chicago 1959); McWhiney, G and Jamieson, P D **Attack and Die** (University of Alabama, 1982); **Military Analysis of the Civil War** (Millwood New York 1977 - collection of articles from **Military Affairs**, notably Mahon's **Infantry Assault Tactics**); Wagner, A L **Organization and Tactics** (New York 1895).

## MEMOIRS

The Civil War is probably the richest war ever fought when it comes to personal memoirs, regimental histories by participants and published volumes of letters from the front. It would be useless to begin to list these here, except to mention that Sherman's **Memoirs** (new edn, 2 Vols, London England 1875, conclusion to Vol 2) is the single most informative document for the technical side of generalship. Good recent anthologies of 'snippets' include Commager, H S **The Blue and the Gray** (2 Vols, Indianapolis 1950); Eisenschiml, O and Newman, R **The American Iliad** (New York 1947); Wiley, B I **The Life of Johnny Reb** (Indianapolis 1943) and **The Life of Billy Yank** (Louisiana State University 1952).

## SPECIALIST BRANCHES OF THE SERVICE

Adams, G W **Doctors in Blue** (New York 1952 - medical aspects); Halleck H W **Elements of Military Art and Science** (1846, reprinted Westport Conn. 1971 - for staff, command and engineering); Naisawald, L V L **Grape and Canister** (Oxford University 1960 - field artillery of the Army of the Potomac); Rogers, H C B **The Confederates and Federals at War** (London England 1973 - staff, command and organizational aspects); Shannon, F A **The Organization and Administration of the Union Army** (2 Vols 1928, reprinted Gloucester Mass. 1965); Starr, S Z **The Union Cavalry in the Civil War** (Louisiana State University, 3 Vols 1979-85); Wise, J C **The Long Arm of Lee** (1915 reissued Oxford University Press 1959 - the field artillery of the Army of Northern Virginia).

## HARDWARE

Coggins, J **Arms and Equipment of the Civil War** (New York 1962); Edwards, W B **Civil War Guns** (Harrisburg Pa. 1962); Fuller, C E and Steuart, R D **Firearms of the Confederacy** (Huntington, West Virginia 1944); Lewis, B R **Small Arms and Ammunition in the U S Service 1776-1865** (Washington DC 1956); Lord, F A **They Fought for the Union** (New York 1960) and **Civil War Collector's Encyclopaedia** (Harrisburg Pa. 1963); Thomas D S **Ready-Aim-Fire!** (Biglerville Pa. 1981 - excellent analysis of small arms and ammunition at Gettysburg); Weller, J **Shooting Confederate Infantry Arms** in **The American Rifleman** (April, May & June 1954); Zimmermann, R J **Unit Organization in the American Civil War** (Cambridge, Ontario 1982).